To Andrew Palmer,
founder of the New Covent Garden Soup Company,
who had a very good idea and against the odds,
made it happen.

NEW COVENT GARDEN SOUP COMPANY'S
Book of Soups

NEW, OLD & ODD RECIPES

Caroline Jeremy
Marketing Director

Fiona Gedd
Public Relat
Manager

Stewart Mackay
Business
Development
Manager

George Jamieson
Warehouse Manager

William Kendall
Managing Director

Nigel Rose
Factory
Development
Assistant

John Stapleton
Production
Director

Samantha Blake
Factory Manager

Nina Bahd
Accounts Assistant

Sarah Randell
Product Development
Assistant

Jane Dodd
Commercial Manager

Mahesh Desai
Production Manager

Alison Adcock
Product Development Manager

NEW COVENT GARDEN SOUP COMPANY'S

Book of Soups

NEW, OLD & ODD RECIPES

Editor: Fiona Geddes

B🌿XTREE

EDITOR'S FOREWORD

I joined the New Covent Garden Soup Company as Public Relations Manager in January 1995 because I loved their soups. Always a great fan of homemade food that you don't have to make, I am the typical gourmet who has only limited cooking skills. However, I still optimistically believe that anyone can cook anything if they follow a good recipe, despite having my fair share of disasters. When collecting recipes for this book, I have chosen ones that really do look and taste delicious (my favourite word) but are not complicated. We have valiantly tasted up to 30 soups a day to make sure that they are as good as we can get them and this has been an education in itself. I have tried all sorts of new flavours including those that did not appeal - for you, reader, I have forced down fresh oyster - and they were all a pleasant surprise. Like everybody else at the soup company, I strongly believe that fresh, simple, unadulterated food is the best and the soups in this book bear this out. If like me, your cooking does not quite match your own gourmet expectations, homemade soup is a very good place to start.

Fiona Geddes
4 June 1996

ACKNOWLEDGEMENTS

Executive Editor: Caroline Jeremy

Editor: Fiona Geddes

Designer: Claire Fry

Illustrations: Katherine McEwen

Recipes tested by: Jo Gilks
Assisted by: Rachael Adcock
Further testing: Sarah Hooley, Fiona Turner, Tizzy Short, Kate Duckett, Gilly Booth

Grateful thanks to: All the contributors, Michael, Vicky, Christine, Ian and Sarah at Boxtree,
David and Margaret Slater, Paul Geddes,
Julia and Eleanor at Phipps PR, Katie, Alison, Kate, Sarah and Nikki and everybody else at NCGSCo.
New Covent Garden Soup Company, 35 Hythe Road, London NW10 6RS

First published in Great Britain in 1999 by Boxtree Ltd, London

This edition published 1998 by Boxtree
an imprint of Pan Macmillan Ltd
Pan Macmillan, 20 New Wharf Road, London N1 9RR
Basingstoke and Oxford
Associated companies throughout the world
www.panmacmillan.com

ISBN 0 7522 0503 X

CONTENTS

All recipes marked (**V**) are suitable for vegetarians
This only applies to soups not garnishes

'There are thick soups,
thin and elegant soups,
fish soups and simple soups,
fruit and wine soups;
so much variety'

The International Wine and Food Society's Guide to Soups, Robin Howe, 1967

INTRODUCTION

'The fact is that fresh vegetables cooked in clean water count among the sublime things in the world'

*Soups from The Good Cook/Techniques and Recipes series by
Richard Olney & others Time Life Books 1979*

ck in the mid 1980s, a revolution was taking place in the type of food you could buy in
permarkets. For the first time we were being offered, in the chilled cabinets, food that tasted like
had been made at home. Against this background, the New Covent Garden Soup Company was
nceived. It seemed strange that a perfectly delicious soup could be made by an ordinary cook in
eir own kitchen provided that they used good ingredients, yet the only soup available in the shops
s a highly processed kind – useful enough in an emergency but by no means as good. If the
permarkets were interested in new, fresher products, then maybe there was a chance for a tiny
ganisation to have a look in. It was this rather simple analysis which persuaded Andrew Palmer,
r company's founder, that his idea of homemade quality soup, made on a large scale, would work.

e legend, which just happens to be true, goes like this: Andrew had been on a particularly
acherous sailing trip and returned to his parents' home cold and wet. As it was summer, his mother
d made salad for lunch but, while lying in the bath (where, incidentally, some of history's best ideas
ve been generated), Andrew called down to her that he would prefer one of her delicious home-
ade soups. Mrs Palmer replied that she had not made any. This caused Andrew to wonder why no
memade-quality soup was available to buy in the shops and suddenly the idea which was to become
e New Covent Garden Soup Company occured to him.

though many people thought the idea was mad, enough friends and friends of friends were
nvinced to put their money behind what we rather grandly called our first factory. This was a
nple affair, more of a large kitchen than a factory. It was designed to make soups which tasted as
od as homemade, with no additives or preservatives in them, yet which lasted long enough for
stomers to want to buy them. It was here that we perfected our methods and our first recipes –
w familiar favourites like Carrot & Coriander. We have come a long way since then but we have
ver been tempted to compromise the basic rules we originally set ourselves – we will only use
gredients that you would find in your own kitchen (so no clever substances like modified starch)
d we will only sell soups we would be happy to serve to our friends. There are plenty of our long
ffering friends out there who will confirm that we pay more than lip service to this latter test.

Marketing experts sometimes tell you that there is no such thing as a bad idea, just bad timing. Whether or not this is the case, there could not have been a better time for us to start than in the late 1980s. There was a growing interest in good food and some frustration that many of the big food manufacturers had failed to spot this. The supermarkets on the other hand could see this change and were happy to try our new ideas. We launched our first range of three flavours – Carrot & Coriander, Vichyssoise and Chicken with Lemon & Tarragon – in 1988. Our soups in their brightly illustrated milk cartons soon had a considerable following and we very quickly had to find a new and bigger place to make them. So in 1990 having persuaded a few more people to lend us some money, we opened a brand new factory in North London and it is here, on the banks of The Grand Union Canal, that we are based today. In 1995, we decided that we needed yet more space to expand, so an old dairy in Peterborough was converted into what is now our second factory.

The New Covent Garden Soup Company started with, and remains, a group of individuals whose first love is good food. As we have grown, however, we have had to learn quickly how to run a successful business. Changing recipes as different vegetables come into season, making and delivering orders to our customers with only a few hours notice and keeping expensive cooking equipment running 24 hours a day; all of this requires people who are more than just good cooks. Yet everybody who works here soon speaks with intimate knowledge of what makes the perfect soup.

Perhaps we should not be surprised that so many different people are interested in good food – it remains one of our basic needs – but I am always amazed by how much time is spent talking about food. As the company grows, we need new people who are passionate about the subject. We seem to attract people who are excited by what we have been doing and who join us with their own set of ideas for us to work on. We always say to ourselves that however much we grow, we must never allow ourselves to turn into just another faceless 'big' company. It was, after all, just this type of organisation that many of us ran away from to join the New Covent Garden Soup Company. This presents no problem as we are constantly encouraged by our enthusiastic newcomers, as well as our growing band of customers, to make a stand for something different and for what we believe in.

Since we started, we have sold over eighty different flavours of soups as well as our newer ranges of sauces and gravies. This is no mean feat in a relatively short history but it represents only a fraction of the number of ideas we have in our recipe book. Not just our own ideas but those we have gleaned from friends, from eating out in restaurants, from competitions we have held, from trips abroad and from the people who grow and sell us our ingredients. In the future we have plans to launch many new recipes, both soups and other dishes, but I am quite sure that we will always have more ideas than the time or space to put them on the supermarket shelves. That is why I am so pleased that, by bringing out the book, we have been able to give more of them the opportunity to be tasted. All of us at The New Covent Garden Soup Company have thoroughly enjoyed tasting the following recipes although deciding which ones should go in has provoked some heated debate.
I hope you agree with our choices.

William Kendall
Managing Director
New Covent Garden Soup Company

'Anyone who can cut up a vegetable can make a soup in a little more time than it takes to open a tin of soup and heat it up'

Soups from The Good Cook/Techniques and Recipes series by Richard Olney & others Time Life Books 1979

TRICKS OF THE TRADE

s you will find when reading this book, the history of each soup is as exciting, interesting and varied the eating.

ll soups from the plain to the exotic, have interesting origins; they are reflections of the people that ake them. It is the life and experience of the cook, which gives each soup its individual character.

ven after tasting forty-eight soups at one session we have still felt inspired to dip our spoons once ore and the exclamations of ecstacy have never ceased to flow.

ome of our greatest downs and ups during our ten year forage into soups have been caused by gredients: customers poised for a launch while the kohlrabi tells us by its size that it would like to ay in the ground for three more weeks; burning tears for anyone entering the spice store when the est batch of pepper is extra hot; sixty tons of butternut, that decided to rot before it had even left ew Zealand; and Jerusalem Artichokes, ugly, delicious and impossible to clean.

he year round availability of vegetables helps us in our quest to give our customers variety, but also uses complications. The home cook should follow the seasons and their produce, but if using ported ingredients should select the more robust vegetables and fruits which can better withstand ld storage, ripening off the bush, and transportation.

he key to any soup is its ingredients. When we have ideas, whether in a flash while doing some odd ore or in a more formal setting with new recipes as the focus, it is so often one particular vegetable ingredient which triggers the character for a soup.

ne of the most exciting things about soup is it can be made from almost anything. It allows those serted or forgotten vegetables a chance to be transformed provided they are fresh.

HICCUPS

There are some hiccups which occur again and again!

- Cream or milk can add richness, and a velvety texture, but too much can overpower the flavour of vegetables and destroy the distinctive flavour of any soup.

- Before adding any dairy ingredients, but especially yoghurt, to a soup, make sure you have allowed it to cool down first, otherwise it will curdle.

- Salt is often used in great quantities during cooking, so that the flavours of the key ingredients instead of being enhanced, are destroyed and impossible to identify. The flatness of a soup which has been overseasoned is one of our bugbears and we believe that if some of the seasoning is left to just before serving, the true flavour of the ingredients are given a lift which is fresh and light.

- Spices are so often treated in a haphazard and crude way. Ideally you need to crush and mix them yourself, but if you are using ready-mixed spices the least you should do is use freshly-opened or well-sealed ones. Many of us, if honest, would have to admit to not storing spices correctly and having piles of half-opened packets lying around date less in disarray. Spices should always be properly cooked otherwise they will give off a harsh, unpleasant flavour which can spoil even the most delicious food.

- It is preferable to thicken a soup using potatoes, bread, pasta, an egg-based mixture or more vegetables, rather than flour which tends to be less controllable and can spoil the texture of some soups.

- One of our most important tasks is to check that the taste and texture of the soups we make do not change over time. A soup made today will always be different to the same one that was made yesterday, and some will change more than others. Often the soups which have a more complicated blend of flavours improve over time whereas the simpler soups which rely more on one vegetable are best eaten immediately.

- Texture can make or break a soup and often it is the tool which is to blame. We prefer to use a blender as it seems to give a fluffier more velvet-like texture. Food processors and handheld blenders do not produce the best results.

- Undercooking and overcooking can destroy. If you are not happy with what you have made it is always worth considering whether you have given the soup enough cooking time for the flavours to develop or the meats to become tender. Overcooking is a trap many of us still fall into. Some of the simpler soups require a minimum cooking time and once that moment has passed, the soup is in decline.

Caroline Jeremy

Caroline Jeremy
Marketing Director
New Covent Garden Soup Company

Stocks

'Since time immemorial
country people the world over
have kept the stockpot simmering
all day long on the kitchen stove'

The International Wine and Food Society's Guide to Soups,
Robin Howe, 1987 The Cookery Book Club

Speak to anyone about soups and it is stocks that seem to daunt them. We have even met professional cooks who have resorted to stock cubes because the idea of making a stock seems to present a problem.

The stock is the key to a good soup, and is, in turn, dependent on the quality of its ingredients. The secret is to leave it undisturbed, save for the occasional skimming of impurities. Once you are familiar with the routine, it can almost become therapeutic!

Stock will transform almost any dish, so it is worth making more than you need and freezing the remainder.

The following recipes make larger quantities than you will need for most of the soups in the book.

Vegetable Stock

PREPARATION TIME: 20 minutes
COOKING TIME: 1 hour 45 minutes
MAKES: 2.7 litres (4½ pints)

3 medium onions, roughly chopped
5 medium carrots, roughly chopped
3 medium leeks, coarsely sliced
3 medium sticks celery, roughly chopped
8 cabbage leaves, sliced
1 head of full flavoured
   green lettuce, sliced
6 sprigs of fresh flat-leaf parsley
   with stems, roughly chopped
3 sprigs of fresh thyme
1 bay leaf
a pinch of salt
3.5 litres (6 pints) cold water to cover

Place all the ingredients in a saucepan or stockpot. Cover and bring slowly to the boil. Reduce heat to a gentle simmer. Skim off any scum. Simmer very gently with the lid ajar for one hour, skimming from time to time. Do not disturb the stock or move it in any way. Strain well. Be careful not to force any of the ingredients through the sieve, as this will cloud the stock. Allow to cool. Refrigerate.

Chicken Stock

PREPARATION TIME : 15 minutes
COOKING TIME : RICH STOCK : 3 hours
LIGHT STOCK : 1½- 2 hours
MAKES : 2.25 litres (4 pints)

1.5 Kg (3lb 2oz) fresh chicken
1 medium onion stuck with 3 cloves
2 medium carrots, coarsely sliced
2 medium sticks celery, coarsely sliced
unpeeled cloves of 1 head of garlic
6 sprigs of fresh flat- leaf parsley with stems
3 sprigs of fresh thyme
1 bay leaf
a pinch of salt
3 litres (5¼ pints) cold water to cover
     by at least 7.5cm (3in)

Place all the ingredients in a saucepan or stockpot. Cover
and bring slowly to the boil. Reduce heat to a gentle
simmer. Skim off any scum. Simmer very gently with the
lid ajar for 2-3 hours for a rich stock and for 1½- 2
hours for a light stock, skimming from time to time.
Do not disturb the stock or move it in any way. Strain
well. Be careful not to force any of the ingredients
through the sieve. Allow to cool. Refrigerate. Skim off
any fat.

Fish Stock

PREPARATION TIME: 25 minutes
COOKING TIME: 1 hour
MAKES: 2 litres (3½ pints)

1 Kg (2lb 2oz) fish bones, heads and trimmings from non-oily fish, broken up and rinsed under cold water
1 medium onion, roughly chopped
2 medium carrots, coarsely sliced
1 medium leek, coarsely sliced
1 medium stick celery, coarsely sliced
¼ head of Florence fennel, sliced
3 sprigs of fresh flat-leaf parsley with stems
3 sprigs of fresh thyme
1 bay leaf
a pinch of salt
2.5 litres (4¾ pints) cold water to cover

Place all the ingredients in a saucepan or stockpot. Cover and bring slowly to the boil. Reduce heat to a gentle simmer. Skim off any scum. Simmer very gently with the lid ajar for 30 minutes, skimming from time to time. Do not disturb the stock or move it in any way. Strain well. Be careful not to force any of the ingredients through the sieve. Allow to cool. Refrigerate.

Fish stock does not need as much simmering as other stocks. Too much cooking will result in the bones giving off a bitter flavour.

Beef Stock

PREPARATION TIME: 1 hour
COOKING TIME: 3½ hours
MAKES: 3 LITRES (5 pints)

3.7 kg (8lb) beef bones (shin, leg or ribs)
6 litres (10½ pints) water to cover
1 tablespoon sunflower oil
2 small onions, halved and unskinned
2 medium carrots, coarsely sliced
2 medium leeks, coarsely sliced
a few fresh parsley stalks
2 small sprigs of fresh thyme
2 bay leaves
15 black peppercorns
a pinch of salt

If you would like a dark stock, pre-heat the oven to 200°C/ 400°F / Gas Mark 6 and roast the bones in a roasting tin for about 30-40 minutes until well browned, and then proceed with the recipe below.

Wash the bones well, then put them into a large saucepan or stockpot with the water. Cover and bring slowly to the boil. Reduce the heat to a gentle simmer. Skim off any scum. Simmer very gently with the lid ajar for about 1½ hours, skimming from time to time.

Meanwhile, heat the oil and sauté the onions over a moderate heat until well browned, but do not burn. Add them to the bones and water, together with the remaining ingredients. Bring back to the boil. Reduce the heat to a gentle simmer. Skim off any scum. Simmer very gently with the lid ajar for another 2 hours, skimming from time to time. Do not disturb the stock or move it in any way. Strain well. Be careful not to force any of the ingredients through the sieve. Allow to cool. Refrigerate. Skim off any fat.

If you would like a richer stock with more depth of flavour, once the stock has been refrigerated and the fat removed, put it into a clean saucepan and simmer until it is reduced by evaporation to the required strength.

Game Stock

PREPARATION TIME: 40 minutes
COOKING TIME: 2 hours 30 minutes
MAKES: 2 litres (3½ pints)

1.5 kg (3lb 5oz) scraps and bones of the roasted or
    fresh carcasses of 2 pheasants or other game
3 – 4 medium onions, quartered
2 medium carrots, coarsely sliced
1 turnip, coarsely sliced (optional)
a small bunch of fresh parsley stalks
1 tablespoon whole allspice
2 teaspoons black peppercorns
1 bay leaf
a pinch of salt
3 litres (5 pints) of cold water to cover

Place all the ingredients in a large saucepan or stockpot.
Cover and bring to the boil. Reduce the heat to a gentle
simmer. Skim off the scum. Simmer very gently with the
lid ajar for 3 hours, skimming from time to time. Do not
disturb the stock or move in any way. Strain well.
Be careful not to force any of the ingredients through
the sieve. Allow to cool. Refrigerate. Skim off any fat.

CHAPTER ONE

Wonderful

'Beautiful Soup so rich and green,
Waiting in a hot tureen!
Who for such dainties would not stoop?
Soup of the evening, beautiful soup!
Beautiful Soup! Who cares for fish,
Game or any other dish?
Who would not give all else for two
Pennyworth only of beautiful soup'

Alice's Adventures in Wonderland, Lewis Carroll 1865

Carrot & Coriander Soup

Created from a suggestion by Andrew Palmer who founded the New Covent Garden Soup Company, this was the first fresh soup ever to be made for sale and has been the most popular ever since. The recipe was originally made with chicken stock but was changed to vegetable after we received many letters from vegetarian soup lovers who felt excluded.

PREPARATION AND COOKING TIME: 40 minutes
SERVES: 6

25g (1oz) butter
1 medium onion, finely chopped
1 garlic clove, crushed
550g (1¼lb) carrots, of which
    450g (1lb) roughly chopped, and
    110g (4oz) coarsely grated
1 litre (1¾ pints) vegetable stock (see page 6)
a pinch of freshly grated nutmeg
1 tablespoon chopped fresh coriander
150ml (¼ pint) single cream
salt and freshly ground black pepper

TO GARNISH:
150ml (¼ pint) yoghurt
2 tablespoons chopped fresh coriander

Melt the butter and cook the onion and garlic gently until soft in a covered saucepan, without colouring. Add the roughly chopped carrots, stock and nutmeg. Cover, bring to the boil and simmer gently until the vegetables are tender. Cool a little, then purée in a liquidiser. Return the soup to a clean saucepan and stir in the grated carrots, coriander and cream. Taste for seasoning. Serve garnished with a swirl of yoghurt and a sprinkling of chopped fresh coriander.

Russian Vegetable Soup

A photocopied page of a cook book turned up in our cuttings scrapbox which included this unusual recipe. It turned out to be a very creative, alternative version of vegetable soup which is much more exciting than the ordinary ingredients suggest. It was no surprise, therefore, to discover that the recipe came from The Cranks Recipe Book. Cranks, the famous vegetarian restaurateurs, are renowned for their wholesome and healthy dishes, so this soup is probably very good for you as well.

PREPARATION AND COOKING TIME: 50 minutes
SERVES: 6

50g (2oz) butter
1 medium onion, finely chopped
225g (8oz) potatoes, peeled and sliced
110g (4oz) parsnips, sliced
110g (4oz) carrots, sliced
50g (2oz) cabbage, finely sliced
2 tablespoons freshly chopped flat-leaf parsley
½ teaspoon dried mixed herbs
freshly grated nutmeg to taste
1.2 litres (2 pints) vegetable stock (see page 6)
salt and freshly ground black pepper

TO GARNISH:
1 small leek, cut into 5cm (2in) strips

Melt half of the butter and cook the vegetables gently for 10 minutes in a covered saucepan, without colouring. Add the parsley, herbs, nutmeg and stock. Cover, bring to the boil and simmer gently for 30 minutes. Cool a little, then purée in a liquidiser. Taste for seasoning.

Meanwhile, fry the leek strips in the remaining butter until crisp. Drain on kitchen paper.

Reheat the soup and serve garnished with the crisp leek strips.

Reproduced with the permission of Orion Books
from The Cranks Recipe Book by Cranks Restaurants

Pappa al Pomodoro

Kate Raison, the soup company's Marketing Manager, keeps the soup company up-to-date with what's current in food through her extra-curricular and unpaid research around London's restaurant scene. Not given to eating in, Kate samples the wares of the capital's most fashionable eateries by night and reviews them for the benefit of the office the next day. A fan of Italian food, one of Kate's favourite haunts is the River Café, situated by the Thames at Hammersmith. Run by Ruth Rogers and Rose Gray, the Café is very well regarded for its authentic Italian food and its bestselling cookbook. This is a recipe from that book which both Kate and the authors cite as their favourite soup.

PREPARATION AND COOKING TIME: 1 hour
SERVES: 6

175ml (6 fl oz) extra virgin olive oil
4 garlic cloves, cut into fine slivers
4 kg (9lb) ripe tomatoes, skinned, quartered and seeded or
    2 kg (4½lb) tinned plum tomatoes, drained of most of their juices
salt and freshly ground black pepper
sugar to taste
2 loaves stale pugliese bread or other open textured
  white bread made with olive oil
1 large bunch fresh basil

TO GARNISH:
extra virgin olive oil
6 small sprigs of fresh basil

Warm the oil and cook the garlic gently for a few minutes. Just as the garlic begins to brown, add the tomatoes. Simmer uncovered for 20-30 minutes, stirring occasionally, until the tomatoes become concentrated. Taste for seasoning, and, if necessary, add sugar to taste. Add 570ml (1pint) water and bring to the boil.

Cut off most of the crust of the bread and break the remaining bread into large pieces. Add the bread to the tomato mixture and stir until the bread absorbs the liquid, adding more boiling water if it is too thick. Remove from the heat and allow to cool a little.

If the basil leaves are large, tear them into pieces, then stir into the soup with 110-175ml (4-6 fl oz) extra virgin olive oil. Allow to sit for 10 minutes before serving to allow the bread to absorb the flavour of the basil and oil. To serve, drizzle olive oil on top and garnish with sprigs of fresh basil.

Roasted Tomato Soup with Basil Purée

Roasting vegetables makes them sweeter and their flavour more intense – even the most insipid of tomatoes (and there are lots of those around) perk up with a good roast. To me, the title of this soup sounds absolutely delicious and the flavour is no disappointment.

PREPARATION AND COOKING TIME: 1 hour 15 minutes
SERVES: 6

1.8 Kg (4lb) ripe tomatoes
200 ml (7 floz) extra virgin olive oil
6 large garlic cloves, crushed
4 bay leaves
4 sprigs of fresh thyme
4 sprigs of fresh rosemary
4 medium onions, finely sliced
4 sticks celery, sliced
1 medium head of fennel, sliced
½ fresh red chilli, deseeded, or to taste
2 teaspoons tomato purée
2 teaspoons sugar
juice of 1 lemon
salt

BASIL PURÉE
60g (2½ oz) fresh basil leaves
½ teaspoon salt
4 tablespoons extra virgin olive oil
2 teaspoons balsamic vinegar

CIABATTA CROÛTONS
4 medium slices of ciabatta bread
1 tablespoon extra virgin olive oil
1 dessertspoon olive paste.

TO GARNISH:
a little good olive oil
6 small sprigs fresh flat-leaf parsley or thyme

Pre-heat the grill. Cut the tomatoes in half and place cut side up on a baking sheet. Grill until soft and beginning to darken at the edges. Remove from the grill and pre-heat the oven to 190°C/375°F/Gas Mark 5.

Heat the olive oil with the garlic and herbs in a large saucepan. When hot, add all the other vegetables. Cook over a moderate heat for a few minutes, stirring now and then, until the vegetables begin to soften, then transfer to a roasting tin and roast in the oven for 30 minutes until soft. Remove from the oven and purée in a liquidiser with the the tomatoes, tomato purée, sugar and lemon juice. Add water if necessary to make a smooth pouring consistency. Pass through a sieve into a clean pan. Taste for seasoning and add more water if necessary.

To make basil purée, pound the basil leaves with the salt in a pestle and mortar until smooth. Add the olive oil and balsamic vinegar and stir well. If you do not have a pestle and mortar, purée all the ingredients in a liquidiser.

To make the croûtons, cut the ciabatta into 2cm (¾in) dice and toss with olive oil and olive paste in a bowl. Arrange on a baking tray in a single layer, then bake for 8-10 minutes.

Reheat the soup and serve each bowl with a heaped teaspoon of basil purée on top and a few ciabatta croûtons. Garnish each bowl with the oil and sprigs of herbs.

Jerusalem Artichoke and Carrot Soup

This velvety deep-flavoured soup was the winner of our first Good Housekeeping Competition in 1994. The recipe was created by Pennie Bennett from London who saw the potential of Jerusalem artichokes as a soup ingredient- they are both nutritious and full of fibre. Alone in a soup they have a rather strong and unfamilar flavour but combined with the sweetness of carrot, the result is a classic. First made by us as a Soup of the Month in 1994, the recipe now has a firm place in our winter range.

PREPARATION AND COOKING TIME: 35 minutes
SERVES: 6

25g (1oz) butter
1 medium onion, finely chopped
400g (14oz) Jerusalem artichokes, peeled and chopped
450g (1lb) carrots, of which
    240g (8½ oz) roughly chopped
    110g (4oz) grated
½ stick celery, roughly chopped
900ml (1½ pints) vegetable stock (see page 6)
110ml (4 floz) milk
salt and freshly ground black pepper

TO GARNISH:
1 tablespoon sunflower oil
3 rashers unsmoked streaky bacon, chopped
150ml (¼ pint) single cream

Melt the butter and cook the onion gently until soft in a covered saucepan, without colouring. Add the artichokes, roughly chopped carrots and celery and cook gently for 2 minutes. Add the vegetable stock, cover and bring to the boil. Simmer gently for about 20 minutes until the vegetables are tender.

Meanwhile, heat the oil for the garnish and sauté the chopped bacon over a moderate heat until crisp. Drain on kitchen paper.

Cool the soup a little, then purée in a liquidiser. Return to a clean saucepan and stir in the grated carrots and milk. Season. Cover and simmer gently for a further 5 minutes. Serve garnished with a swirl of single cream and sprinkled with crisp bacon.

National Trust Wild Mushroom Soup

New Covent Garden Soup Company are sponsoring a National Trust garden by donating 10p from the sale price of every carton of this soup. Fenton House, built in 1698, is a small but beautiful property in Hampstead with walled grounds that border Hampstead Heath. The grounds include a rose garden, an orchard, a vegetable garden and borders. Our money will be used to build a vinehouse where one originally stood, put in an irrigation system and replace terracotta borders. Wild Mushroom was chosen as a flavour as they were picked on Hampstead Heath in the seventeenth and eighteenth centuries. Sales of this sophisticated soup have been so good, that we hope to contribute £40,000. Look out for stories of the garden's progress in gardening magazines.

PREPARATION AND COOKING TIME: 50 minutes
SERVES: 6

75g (3oz) dried cep mushrooms
300ml (11 floz) warm water
50g (2oz) butter
2 medium onions, finely chopped
2 garlic cloves, crushed
225g (8oz) chestnut mushrooms, sliced
2 dessertspoons plain flour
900ml (1½ pints) vegetable stock (see page 6)
150ml (¼ pint) dry white wine
2 dessertspoons finely chopped fresh flat-leaf parsley
225ml (8 floz) single cream
salt and freshly ground black pepper

TO GARNISH:
150ml (¼ pint) natural yoghurt

Soak the ceps in the warm water for 20 minutes. Drain, reserving the soaking liquor.

Melt the butter and cook the onions and garlic gently for 10 minutes in a covered saucepan, without colouring. Add the mushrooms and ceps and cook for 2 minutes. Stir in the flour and cook for 2 minutes. Gradually add the stock, the reserved soaking liquor and the white wine. Cover, bring to the boil and simmer gently for about 20 minutes until the vegetables are tender. Cool a little, then add the parsley and purée in a liquidiser. Return to a clean saucepan, stir in the cream and reheat gently. Season to taste and serve garnished with a swirl of natural yoghurt.

Fiorentine Bean Soup

Valentina Harris, the doyenne of Italian cookery, gives this recipe for an authentic bean soup, Zuppa Fagiola alla Fiorentina, in her book, Italian Regional Cookery, 1990. Although it sounds similar to our Tuscan Bean, it is, in fact, quite different. The key to its intense flavour is the infusion of herbs into the olive oil. Leftover soup can be used to make the famous Italian dish 'Ribollita' (which means 'reboiled') by adding bread and olive oil so the consistency becomes thick and stew-like.

PREPARATION AND COOKING TIME: 1 hour 40 minutes plus the soaking of the beans overnight

SERVES: 6

1kg (2lb 2oz) fresh or 450g (1lb) dried cannellini or borlotti beans, washed
8 tablespoons extra virgin olive oil
5 large garlic cloves, of which
  2 should be peeled and chopped,
  2 should be crushed without peeling, and
  1 should be peeled only
2 large onions, finely chopped
1 carrot, chopped
1 leek, chopped
1 stick celery, chopped
1 large ripe tomato, peeled, deseeded and chopped
1 ham bone
1.5 litres (2¾ pints) water
salt
½ teaspoon beef extract
275g (10oz) dark green cabbage leaves (ideally the black Tuscan cabbage cavolo nero), cut into large pieces
1 sprig fresh rosemary
a pinch of dried thyme

TO GARNISH:

6 slices coarse white bread
5 tablespoons freshly grated Parmesan cheese

If using dried beans, soak them overnight and boil twice for 5-10 minutes, washing in between each boil. Drain.

Heat 3 tablespoons of olive oil and cook the 2 chopped garlic cloves and the onions for 5 minutes in a covered saucepan, without colouring. Add the remaining vegetables, the ham bone, beans and water. Add a pinch or two of salt and the beef extract. Cover, bring to the boil and simmer gently for about 1 hour until the beans are tender.

Remove the ham bone and 1 large ladleful of whole, cooked beans, then purée the remaining soup in a liquidiser. Return the soup to a clean pan with the reserved beans. Stir in the cabbage. Cover and simmer gently for about 10 minutes, until the cabbage is tender.

Meanwhile, pour the remaining olive oil into a small saucepan and heat it gently with the rosemary, thyme and the 2 unpeeled but crushed garlic cloves. After about 10 minutes, strain the oil into the soup and heat it through for 3 minutes, stirring constantly. Toast the bread in the oven. Rub each side of the toast with the remaining peeled garlic clove. Put the toast in the base of each bowl. Ladle over the soup, then sprinkle with Parmesan cheese.

This recipe is reproduced from Valentina Harris' Italian Regional Cookery, published by BBC Books

Soupe de Poissons

An authentic French fish soup, based on our award-winning carton version. This beautiful terracotta soup, as eaten in the South of France, must be eaten with its three traditional garnishes: French bread croûtons, Gruyère cheese and rouille or aïoli. Caroline Jeremy, who developed many of the original flavours, remembers having to get this one right over the hottest weekend of 1990 in her small flat in Balham. Due to the urgency of the work, she had to miss her friends engagement party and had to suffer her boyfriend coming home at eleven o'clock, drunk and sunburnt after having had a great time at the all-day celebration. To add insult to injury, the smell of fish lingered stubbornly around her flat for several days to remind her.

PREPARATION AND COOKING TIME: 1 hour 20 minutes
SERVES: 6

900g (2lb) fish and shellfish, e.g. bass, bream, sole carcasses, crab etc.
3 tablespoons extra virgin olive oil
1 large leek, finely sliced
1 medium onion, finely sliced
½ medium head of Florence fennel, finely sliced
8 large garlic cloves, chopped
225g (8oz) tomatoes, chopped
1 bay leaf
rind of ½ orange, cut into very fine strips
salt and freshly ground black pepper
a pinch of saffron shreds combined with 1 tablespoon warm water

FOR THE ROUILLE:
110g (4oz) red pepper
½ small fresh red chilli, or to taste
8 garlic cloves, peeled
2 teaspoon chopped fresh thyme or basil
salt

FOR THE AÏOLI
8-10 garlic cloves, peeled
2 egg yolks, beaten well
salt and freshly ground white pepper
juice of 1 lemon
1 teaspoon Dijon mustard
275ml (½ pint) oil
(½ groundnut and ½ olive oil)

Wash the fish and pat dry with kitchen paper. Fillet and skin the fish if necessary and cut into large pieces. Remove any shellfish from their shells.

Heat the oil and cook the leek, onion, fennel and garlic gently for 10 minutes in a covered saucepan, without colouring. Add the tomatoes, bay leaf and orange strips and taste for seasoning. Cook for a further 5 minutes. Add the fish, then cover with boiling water. Simmer vigorously for 5 minutes, then break up the fish with a wooden spoon to extract the flavours. Simmer the broth for 30 minutes, stirring occasionally. Pass the soup through a fine sieve, pressing hard with a wooden spoon to squeeze out all the fish juices, but do not grind the solids through the sieve. Return the broth to a clean saucepan. Bring to the boil and stir in the saffron.

For the rouille, purée all the ingredients in a liquidiser. For the aïoli, purée the garlic, yolks, salt and pepper, lemon juice and mustard in a liquidiser. With the machine running, gradually add the oil until a thick, shiny, firm sauce is obtained.

Reheat the soup gently, float the croûtons coated with rouille or aïoli on top of the soup and then sprinkle with grated Gruyère cheese.

Jane Dodd's Borscht

Jane is our Commercial Manager and is responsible for buying in the best ingredients at the best prices. She was a founder member of the soup company and epitomises the perfect New Covent Garden Soup Company employee with a passion for soup. While at university, she used to make soup with her friends in a shared student house. They had no blender so they used a mouli and she remembers the beetroot-coloured splashes that adorned the walls after a particularly vigorous borscht making session. This borscht however needs no blending - we think the flavours remain more intact without.

PREPARATION AND COOKING TIME: 1 hour 25 minutes
SERVES: 6

500g (1lb 2oz) raw beetroot, peeled and grated
500g (1lb 2oz) red cabbage, finely shredded
3 tablespoons tomato purée
2 tablespoons red wine vinegar
125g (4½oz) butter
1.2 litres (2 pints) beef stock (see page 9)
1 medium onion, grated
1 carrot, grated
salt and freshly ground black pepper
1 tablespoon brown sugar

TO GARNISH:
275ml (½ pint) soured cream

Put the beetroot and red cabbage into a large saucepan. Stir in the tomato purée, vinegar, half the butter and the beef stock. Cover, bring to the boil and simmer gently for 1 hour.

Melt the remaining butter and sauté the onion and carrots until golden. Add to the beetroot and red cabbage mixture. Cover and simmer gently for a further 15 minutes. Taste for seasoning and add the brown sugar. Serve garnished with soured cream.

Moules Marinière

You may not have thought of this recipe as a soup before, but there is no reason why it shouldn't be one. This is our Marketing Director Caroline's recipe, which has never been written down before. Don't worry too much about measuring the ingredients - just dump them all in, make sure you don't overcook the mussels (just until the shells open) and the result will be fine - simple and delicious!

PREPARATION AND COOKING TIME: 40 minutes
SERVES: 6

1.30 Kg (3lb) fresh mussels in their shells
1 tablespoon extra virgin olive oil
3 large shallots, chopped
1 large garlic clove, finely chopped
1 bay leaf
1 sprig fresh thyme
450 ml (¾ pint) dry white wine
275 ml (½ pint) single cream
a large handful finely chopped fresh flat-leaf parsley
salt and freshly ground black pepper

Scrub the mussels under running water and remove any barnacles. Wash very thoroughly 2 or 3 times in plenty of cold water. Drain well.

Heat the oil and cook the shallots, garlic, bay leaf and thyme until soft in a covered saucepan, without colouring. Add the mussels and wine. Cover and put over a high heat. Shake the pan vigorously for about 3-5 minutes, until the mussels have opened. Remove from the heat. Discard any mussels that are still closed.

Toss the mussels in the cream and fresh parsley, season, and serve immediately straight from the saucepan.

Aubergine Soup with Red Pepper Cream

We tried quite a few aubergine soups that tasted rather bitter and came out in an off-putting shade of grey. Jo Gilks, our recipe tester, came to the rescue with this stunning soup: the bright orange red pepper cream contrasts with the purple/grey aubergine purée to give a result that the best interior designer would be proud of – the flavours go really well together too!

PREPARATION AND COOKING TIME: 40 minutes
SERVES: 6

2 tablespoons extra virgin olive oil
450g (1lb) aubergine, coarsely chopped
1 small onion, finely chopped
1 large garlic clove, chopped
1 litre (1¾ pints) light chicken stock (see page 7)
salt and freshly ground black pepper

RED PEPPER CREAM:
1 red pepper, quartered and seeded
2 tablespoons single cream
salt and freshly ground black pepper
chilli oil to taste (optional)

Heat the oil and cook the aubergine, onion and garlic gently for 20 minutes without colouring.

Meanwhile, grill the red pepper until the skin has blackened. Cool in a plastic bag, then skin the pepper and purée with the cream, a seasoning of salt and pepper and chilli oil if you wish.

Cool the aubergine and onion mixture a little and then purée with the stock, salt and pepper. Reheat and spoon the red pepper cream on to the soup just before serving.

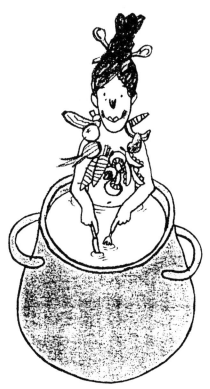

CHAPTER TWO

Unusual

'and broth of abominable things
is in their vessels' *Isaiah Chapter 65 Verse 8*

Callaloo Soup with Coconut

Callaloo is a vegetable leaf grown in the Caribbean that is similar to spinach but has a very interesting and unusual flavour. If you live near London, try getting it at the fascinating Shepherd's Bush Market where it is also sold tinned. This recipe was sent on a postcard from William Kendall, our MD, when he was on holiday in Grenada. Coincidentally, the day before, William had met a man from Harlesden, home of our London factory, under a waterfall on the island.

PREPARATION AND COOKING TIME: 40 minutes
SERVES: 6

2 tablespoons sunflower oil
2 small onions, finely chopped
3 garlic cloves, crushed
2 sprigs of fresh thyme
2 teaspoons finely chopped fresh chives
500g (1lb 2oz) Callaloo or taro leaves
1.2 litres (2 pints) chicken stock (see page 7)
275 - 450 ml (½ - ¾ pint) tinned coconut milk,
          or creamed coconut, to taste
fresh green chilli pepper, seeded to taste
salt and freshly ground black pepper

Heat the oil and cook the onion and garlic gently for 5 minutes in a covered saucepan, without colouring. Add the thyme, chives and taro leaves and cook for 3 minutes, stirring. Add the stock, coconut milk and chilli pepper. Cover, bring to the boil and simmer gently for about 20 minutes until the vegetables are tender. Cool a little, then purée in a liquidiser. Return to a clean saucepan, taste for seasoning and reheat gently. Serve.

Cream of Celeriac Soup

Celeriac is an underrated root vegetable which has the flavour of sweet and nutty celery. Like most root vegetables it is available mainly in winter and forms the basis of this recipe, regularly produced as one of our winter Soups of the Month.

PREPARATION AND COOKING TIME : 40 minutes
SERVES : 6

25g (1oz) butter
400g (14oz) celeriac, peeled and roughly chopped
125g (4½oz) potatoes, peeled and roughly chopped
1 garlic clove, crushed
570ml (1 pint) vegetable stock (see page 6)
1 tablespoon fresh lemon juice
275ml (½ pint) milk
Salt and freshly ground black pepper

Melt the butter and cook the celeriac, potatoes, and garlic gently for 5 minutes without colouring. Add the stock and lemon juice. Bring to the boil and simmer gently until the vegetables are tender. Cool a little, then purée in a liquidiser with the milk. Taste for seasoning. The soup is delicious served both chilled and hot.

New Zealand 'Kumara' or Sweet Potato Chowder

Margaret Quilter really missed the sweet potato soups and chowders that she used to make in her native New Zealand before she came to the UK with her husband in 1971. Finally, the pink-fleshed variety began to appear in British shops and she was inspired to re-create this chowder for one of our recent competitions. Although it is not completely authentic (New Zealand sweet potatoes are parsnip-coloured), Margaret cooks it for her large family, including seven grandchildren, who eat it up 'in a flash'.

PREPARATION AND COOKING TIME: 40 minutes
SERVES: 6

25g (1oz) butter
3 medium onions, sliced
2 ears of corn, flesh removed
570 ml (1 pint) milk
675g (1½lb) sweet potatoes, orange-fleshed if possible, peeled and cut into 2.5 cm (1in) dice
150 ml (¼ pint) double cream

TO GARNISH:
finely chopped fresh flat-leaf parsley
or chopped fresh chives

Melt the butter and cook the onions gently until soft without colouring. In another pan, simmer the corn and the milk for about 20 minutes until tender. Separately, simmer the sweet potatoes for 20 minutes in plenty of salted water until tender. Purée the corn and milk coarsely in a liquidiser with the cream.

Combine the onions, corn mixture and sweet potatoes in a clean saucepan. Reheat and serve sprinkled with parsley or chives.

Roasted Garlic, Turnip and Chervil Soup

Catriona Coghill, a finalist in our Scottish Soup Competition, describes herself as a mother of five, taxi-driver, housewife and hotelier. As the latter, she helps to run a family hotel, the Sligachan, on Skye at the foot of the Cuillins, much beloved by climbers and hill walkers. The hotel restaurant serves mainly seafood and vegetarian cuisine to which Catriona contributes. The inspiration for this original recipe came to her in bed at 4.00am. Having wanted to do something with the turnip, which Catriona feels is much undervalued in Scottish cookery, it suddenly struck her that roasted garlic was the answer she had been looking for. What an excellent idea!

PREPARATION AND COOKING TIME: 1 hour
SERVES: 6

50g (2oz) butter
1 medium onion, finely chopped
4 large garlic cloves, unpeeled and roasted
1 stick celery, finely chopped
1 turnip, about 225g (8oz), grated
225g (8oz) potatoes, peeled and thinly sliced
900ml (1½ pints) light chicken stock (see page 7)
2 tablespoons double cream
2 tablespoons finely chopped fresh chervil
salt and freshly ground black pepper

Melt the butter and cook the onion gently until soft in a covered saucepan, without colouring. Peel the roasted garlic and add to the pan along with the celery, turnip and potatoes. Cook for 2 minutes, then add the stock. Cover, bring to the boil and simmer gently until the vegetables are tender. Cool a little, then purée in a liquidiser. Return to a clean saucepan and reheat gently, adding the cream and chervil. Taste for seasoning and serve.

Roasted Butternut Squash Soup

The New Covent Garden Soup Company is always on the look out for new food fashions as there might be a soup opportunity in them. Sarah, our Marketing Assistant, spotted a trend for butternut squash and bought some to roast. Finding that they were delicious, she mentioned them to Caroline, our Marketing Director, who had happy memories of eating them in South Africa when she was young. Sarah developed a wonderful soup to launch in October 1995 and stocks of butternut were ordered from New Zealand. Sadly, the soup never did get to the shops as all our squashes went bad in the New Zealand warehouse. However, the idea is too good to waste, so the cartoned soup should be available soon. Strangely, the marketing department has a butternut squash as a mascot which sits on Sarah's desk. For some reason, the squash supplier stuck eyes, nose and a tail on the sample he sent us and so far, nobody can bear to throw the creature away.

PREPARATION AND COOKING TIME: 1 hour 10 minutes
SERVES: 6

900g (2lb) butternut squash
40g (1½ oz) butter
350g (12oz) potatoes
1.2 litres (2 pints) vegetable stock (see page 6)
100ml (3½ fl oz) single cream
salt and freshly ground black pepper

TO GARNISH:
3 tablespoons sunflower seeds

Pre-heat the oven to 160°C / 325°F / Gas Mark 3

Cut the butternut squash in half. Scoop out the seeds and discard. Place in a roasting tin and dot with 25g(1oz) of the butter. Bake for about 1 hour until softened and caramelising.

To toast the sunflower seeds, put them into a frying pan over a high heat. Shake the pan frequently until the sunflower seeds brown. Cool.

Melt the remaining butter, add the potatoes and stock and simmer for about 20 minutes until the potatoes are tender.

Allow the butternut squash to cool a little, then scoop the flesh out of its skin and purée with the potato mixture in a liquidiser. Pour into a clean saucepan, stir in the cream and taste for seasoning. Reheat gently and serve garnished with toasted sunflower seeds.

Nettle Soup

Miranda, the wife of our Managing Director, was at university with Vanessa Feltz and, consequently, William is occasionally asked to appear on Vanessa's Talk Radio UK show to talk about soup. During a recent phone-in, Karen, a student of herbal medicine from Edinburgh, told William about the healing properties of nettle soup. Apparently, nettle soup has been eaten in the spring for hundreds of years to cleanse the system of the salty preserved foods traditionally eaten in the winter. It's also rich in iron and Vitamin C. Karen arms herself with rubber gloves and plastic bags and picks the tops off young nettles which grow in sheltered areas away from pollution. Do not be alarmed, cooking totally takes the sting out of the plants and the result is surprisingly good.

PREPARATION AND COOKING TIME: 30 minutes
SERVES: 6

25g (1oz) butter
1 medium onion, finely chopped
2 garlic cloves, crushed
400g (14oz) potatoes, peeled and finely chopped
450g (1lb) freshly picked nettle tops
1 litre (1¾ pints) vegetable stock (see page 6)
150ml (¼ pint) double cream
freshly grated nutmeg
salt and freshly ground black pepper

Melt the butter and cook the onion and garlic gently for 10 minutes in a covered saucepan, without colouring. Add the potatoes and nettles and cook for 2 minutes. Add the stock, cover, bring to the boil and simmer for 15 minutes. Cool a little, then purée in a liquidiser. Return to a clean saucepan, stir in the cream and season with freshly grated nutmeg, salt and pepper to taste. Reheat gently and serve.

Arbroath Smokie and Scottish Cheddar Soup

This soup perfectly answered the brief of our Scottish Soup Competition to create a soup using Scotland's finest ingredients. This was not a difficult task for its creator, Dundee nursery nurse Lynn Salvin who has spent years cooking well balanced, healthy food from fresh, local ingredients to provide wholesome nutrition for her fortunate husband and three children. She is currently trying to encourage Ayley, Jamie and Gregor to learn to cook and appreciate the simple pleasure of preparing and sharing a meal with family or friends. They all eat this delicious creamy soup as a main meal with mashed potatoes.

PREPARATION AND COOKING TIME: 45 minutes
SERVES: 6

50g (2oz) butter
2 medium onions, finely chopped
350g (12oz) potatoes, peeled and chopped
1.2 litres (2 pints) water
1 pair of Arbroath Smokies, skinned, boned and flaked
175g (6oz) mature Scottish Cheddar cheese
125g (4½oz) carrots, coarsely grated
1 green pepper, coarsely grated
2 tablespoons double cream
Salt and freshly ground black pepper

TO GARNISH:
2 tablespoons finely chopped fresh flat-leaf parsley

Melt the butter and cook the onion gently in a covered saucepan until soft, without colouring. Add the potatoes and water. Cover, bring to the boil and simmer gently for 20 minutes until the vegetables are tender. Cool a little, then purée along with two-thirds of the flaked fish. Return to a clean saucepan and reheat gently, stirring in the Cheddar cheese, carrots, green pepper, the remaining flaked fish and the double cream. Taste for seasoning. Serve sprinkled with chopped fresh parsley.

Aussie Roo Soup

Before you recoil in horror, Kangaroo is now available quite widely in the UK and is very similar to beef. One of our recipe testers, Rachel Adcock, who caters for Australian Embassy functions, had some 'roo' left over after the Australia Day celebrations and created this soup for us. We didn't tell anybody at our offices what it was until after they had tried it: the reaction was 100% positive.

PREPARATION AND COOKING TIME: 1 hour
SERVES : 6

75g (3oz) butter
2 medium onions, finely chopped
275g (10oz) Kangaroo meat, finely chopped
3 garlic cloves, crushed
4 medium carrots, chopped
2 large potatoes, about 450g (1lb), peeled and chopped
2 sticks celery, chopped
2 litres (3½ pints) game stock (see page 10,
   using a Kangaroo tail, if you have one to spare)
3 tablespoons finely chopped fresh flat-leaf parsley

To GARNISH:
3 tablespoons garlic croûtons (see page 108
   but first infuse the oil with 1 sliced garlic clove
   before cooking the bread dice)
1 tablespoon sunflower oil
3 rashers unsmoked streaky bacon, chopped

Melt the butter and cook the onion gently for 5 minutes in a covered saucepan, without colouring. Add the kangaroo meat and brown gently. Add all the vegetables, cook for 2 minutes, then add the stock and parsley. Cover, bring to the boil and simmer gently for about 45 minutes until the meat is tender.

For the garnish, heat the oil and sauté the bacon over a moderate heat until crisp. Drain on kitchen paper.

Serve the soup garnished with garlic croûtons and crumbled crisp bacon

Sousboontjie

Pronounced 'sews-boing-key', this soup was sent in to us as an entry to one of our competitions by David Bellamy. He included this description of the soup with his recipe: 'This is a tasty and hearty soup, best eaten with fresh bread to provide a satisfying meal. It is South African in origin, derived from a dish of well cooked and highly spiced beans – sousboontjies – usually eaten with roasted Karoo lamb and glacéed carrots. These beans form part of the traditional Cape cuisine which developed from the kitchens of the original Dutch and Huguenot settlers, whose food would have been prepared by Malaysian cooks taken to South Africa from the Dutch colony. The flavours reflect the 'New World' nature of South African cooking combining French and Dutch cooking styles with the spiciness of Malay cookery'.

PREPARATION AND COOKING TIME: 4 hours
SERVES: 6

400g (14oz) dried red kidney beans, washed
3 litres (5 pints) water
1½ large fresh bay leaves
½ stick cassia, or, if unavailable,
   use cinnamon stick
2 tablespoons extra virgin olive oil
½ teaspoon black mustard seeds
4 garlic cloves, finely chopped
3 large onions, finely chopped
15 grinds of fresh black pepper
4 tablespoons tomato purée
3 teaspoons dried parsley
3 teaspoons chopped fresh thyme
4 leaves fresh rosemary
Juice of ½ lemon
4 tablespoons tamarind purée
Salt

Soak the red kidney beans in plenty of water overnight. Put the beans into a saucepan with the water at least four hours before the soup is to be eaten. Bring to the boil and simmer gently, partially covered, for about two hours, or until the skins come away from the seeds, which will appear to split and become floury.

Using a potato masher, mash one-quarter of the beans in the saucepan. These will thicken the soup. Add the bay leaves and cassia, or cinnamon. Care should be taken not to add too much bay as it may be overpowering.

Heat the oil and add the mustard seeds. When they begin to pop, briefly mash them with the back of a spoon, then add the garlic. Cook over a moderate heat for 2 minutes, stirring and watching that they do not brown. Stir in the onions, grind in the pepper and sauté the onions until golden. Add to the kidney beans and stir well. Add the tomato purée, parsley, thyme and rosemary. Add the two sour ingredients, the lemon juice and tamarind purée. Finally add the salt. Cover and simmer gently for 1 hour, adding more water if necessary to achieve the desired consistency. Serve hot.

Lettuce and Lovage Soup

This soup was inspired by a play called Lettuce and Lovage, starring Maggie Smith, which was put on in London's West End a few years ago. The title reminded us that this old-fashioned combination was due for a revival so we launched it as a Summer soup. Lovage, also known as sea parsley, is an old-fashioned herb that has an intensely celery-like flavour which is sweetened by the lettuce.

PREPARATION AND COOKING TIME: 40 minutes
SERVES: 6

25g (1oz) butter
175g (6oz) spring onions, chopped
250g (9oz) potatoes, peeled and chopped
1.5 kg (3lb 5oz) iceberg lettuce, chopped
570 ml (1 pint) vegetable stock (see page 6)
3 teaspoons lemon juice, or to taste
25g (1oz) chopped fresh lovage leaves
450 ml (3/4 pint) milk
275 ml (1/2 pint) single cream
salt and freshly ground white pepper

TO GARNISH:
6 small sprigs of fresh lovage

Melt the butter and cook the spring onions gently for 5 minutes in a covered saucepan, without colouring. Add the potatoes, lettuce, vegetable stock and lemon juice to taste. Cover, bring to the boil and simmer gently for about 15 minutes until the vegetables are tender. Cool a little, then purée in a liquidiser. Return to a clean pan. Stir in the lovage and simmer gently, covered, for a further 5 minutes. Stir in the milk and cream, season to taste, reheat gently and serve garnished with small sprigs of lovage.

Rich Miso Soup with Garlic

This Japanese influenced soup was sent in by Angela Farnworth of Ledbury, Hertfordshire. Despite having a rich deep flavour, this soup is ultra healthy and suitable for vegans. Miso, fermented soya paste, gives the soup its distinctive flavour – buy the variety that is made with brown rice from specialist Japanese or health food outlets.

PREPARATION AND COOKING TIME: 1 hour 45 minutes
SERVES: 6

FOR THE STOCK:
2 tablespoons extra virgin olive oil
4 medium onions, sliced
9 garlic cloves, peeled
3 medium carrots, chopped
2 sprigs of fresh thyme
¼ teaspoon ground cumin
4 teaspoons tamari or soy sauce
1.75 litres (3 pints) water

2 tablespoons extra virgin olive oil
4 medium onions, finely chopped
2 large garlic cloves, crushed
350g (12oz) potatoes, peeled and chopped
2 medium carrots, chopped
1 teaspoon ground cumin
1 tablespoon tamari or soy sauce
1.2 litres (2 pints) stock (see below)
1 generous dessertspoon brown miso,
    available from specialist shops

For the stock, heat the oil and cook the onion, garlic cloves and chopped carrots gently for 5 minutes in a covered saucepan, without colouring. Add all the remaining stock ingredients, cover, bring to the boil and simmer gently for 1-1½ hours. Strain and make up to 1.2 litres (2 pints) if necessary.

For the soup, heat the oil and cook the onion and garlic gently for 5 minutes in a covered saucepan, without colouring. Add the potatoes, carrots, ground cumin and tamari and cook gently for 5 minutes. Add the reserved stock, cover, bring to the boil and simmer gently for about 30 minutes until the vegetables are tender. Cool a little, then pureé in a liquidiser with the miso. Return to a clean saucepan. Reheat gently and serve.

CHAPTER THREE

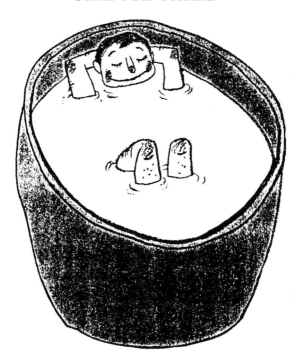

Reviving

'Come to me all of you whose stomachs
cry out and I will restore you'

translation from Latin motto inscribed over the door of
M.Boulanger's soup restaurant opened in Paris in 1765

Soupe au Pistou

A classic soup which could be described as a French version of minestrone. This originates from French peasant cooking but like many such dishes, it is perfectly at home as part of the most sophisticated of meals. Try and use the freshest vegetables possible and don't miss out the pistou, which, like the Italian pesto, is truly blissful in smell and taste when homemade.

PREPARATION AND COOKING TIME: 1 hour 45 minutes
SERVES : 6 as a main course soup

225g (8oz) dried haricot beans
1 small onion, peeled and studded with 2 whole cloves
4 litres (7 pints) water
1 small leek, finely sliced
175g (6oz) carrots, cut into 2cm (3/4 in) dice
110g (4oz) pumpkin, cut into 2cm (3/4 in) dice (optional)
275g (10oz) ripe tomatoes, skinned, deseeded and roughly chopped,
    or 1 x 400g (14oz) tin chopped tomatoes
1 stick celery, cut into 2cm (3/4 in) dice
sprig of thyme
1 bay leaf
225g (8oz) potatoes, peeled and cut into 2cm (3/4 in) dice
175g (6oz) French beans, topped and tailed and cut into 5cm (2in) pieces
110g (4oz) turnip, cut into 2cm (3/4 in) dice
175g (6oz) broad beans
275g (10oz) courgettes, cut into 2cm (3/4 in) dice
50g (2oz) thick vermicelli or elbow macaroni
salt and freshly ground black pepper

FOR THE PISTOU:
4 garlic cloves, peeled
salt
18 large basil leaves
150ml (1/4 pint) extra virgin olive oil
250g (9oz) freshly grated Parmesan cheese

TO GARNISH:
50g (2oz) freshly grated Parmesan cheese
50g (2oz) mature Dutch cheese, grated

Soak the haricot beans overnight in plenty of cold water. Put the clove-stuck onion into a saucepan with the haricot beans and water. Bring to the boil, skim off any scum, then simmer gently for about 30 minutes until the beans are tender. Add the leek, carrots, pumpkin (if using), tomatoes, celery, sprig of thyme and the bay leaf and simmer gently for 15 minutes. Add the potatoes, French beans, turnip and broad beans. Bring the soup to the boil and immediately add the courgettes and vermicelli or macaroni. Taste for seasoning and simmer for 15 minutes, or until the pasta is 'al dente'. Discard the onion and bay leaf.

For the pistou, put the peeled garlic cloves into a liquidiser with a pinch of salt and the basil leaves. Bring to a purée, then slowly add the olive oil. Add the Parmesan cheese and taste for seasoning.

To serve the soup, put the pistou into a tureen and pour in the piping hot soup, stirring all the time. Ladle the soup into bowls and garnish with the mixed Parmesan and Dutch cheese.

Clear Beef Soup with Zupfnockerl

The following is from William Kendall, the soup company's Managing Director:

'Vienna was, until 1918, the centre of an unusually varied empire which covered many culinary traditions. Because of its language, Austria is frequently bracketed with Germany but its culture and cooking is very different. I can not get terribly excited about much German food but in Austria it tends to be lighter, more varied and altogether more exciting. The former empire covered large parts of Northern Italy and much of Eastern Europe so it is hardly surprising. Even the Ottoman Turks reached Vienna's walls and were finally repelled, leaving two quintessentially Viennese things – coffee and strudel.

I have been a frequent traveller in Austria since my youth – for a while I worked as a paper bale weigher in a paper mill near the Hungarian border. I have been a major recipient of Austrian hospitality and have noticed that a lightish soup is frequently served as a first course of a family meal. More often than not it is one of the apparently hundreds of variations on the clear beef soup theme.

The Austrians frequently add different types of noodles, pasta or pancake strips to the soup base. Here I give the Zupfnockerl version – my rather awkward translation is "noodles made by clicking the fingers together".'

PREPARATION AND COOKING TIME: 2 hours 45 minutes
SERVES: 6

1.35 Kg (3lb) beef bones
3.5 litres (5½ pints) water
1 small onion, halved and unskinned
½ medium carrot, coarsely sliced
½ small parsnip, coarsely sliced
1 stick celery, coarsely sliced
½ small leek, coarsely sliced
parsley stalks
10 peppercorns
salt

TO GARNISH:
3 tablespoons chopped fresh chives

FOR THE ZUPFNOCKERL:
200g (7oz) plain flour
2 eggs
pinch of salt
1-2 tablespoons milk
a little melted butter

Wash the bones well, then put them into a large saucepan with the water. Cover, bring to the boil and skim off any scum. Simmer gently, skimming from time to time, for about 1½ hours.

Meanwhile, sauté the onion to a dark brown colour without fat, but do not burn. Add them to the bones and water.

After 1½ hours, add the carrots, parsnip, celery, leek, parsley stalks, peppercorns and salt. Simmer very gently for another 45 minutes, then remove the bones and press the broth and some of the vegetables through a sieve. Reheat and serve either simply with chopped fresh chives or with Zupfnockerl.

To make the Zupfnockerl, mix the ingredients either by hand or in a food processor until a dough is formed. Knead the dough either by hand or in the food processor for 3 minutes. Allow to rest in a plastic bag for 20 minutes, then roll it out to a thickness of 2cm (3/4 in). Bring plenty of salted water to the boil in a large saucepan. Pinch irregular pieces of dough by covering your fingers in flour and clicking them together in the dough. Drop them into the boiling water and remove when they have floated to the surface, about 2-3 minutes. Cool immediately in cold water and drain. When ready to serve the soup, quickly heat them in melted butter and add to the soup.

Italian Peasant Soup

(V)

After leaving the art college where they met, Vanessa and Les Scott renovated a series of houses and cottages. Despite often living in very basic conditions—no windows, unplastered walls, no heating—they never stopped entertaining, which provoked Vanessa's father to comment: 'Why don't you put a hotel sign up outside and start charging?'. Six years later the couple are now happily ensconced in their own small country hotel 'Strattons' in the market town of Swaffham in Norfolk with their children and a menagerie of animals. Vanessa loves cooking and this recipe, which she entered for one of our competitions, was inspired by a very memorable family meal in Italy.

PREPARATION AND COOKING TIME: 45 minutes
SERVES: 6

4 tablespoons extra virgin olive oil
2 medium onions, finely chopped
400g (14oz) potatoes, peeled and diced
1 bulb of Florence fennel, sliced
110g (4oz) carrots, diced
3 large garlic cloves, crushed
1 tablespoon sun-dried tomato paste
½ medium red pepper, deseeded and finely diced
1.2 litres (2 pints) vegetable stock (see page 6)
450g (1lb) ripe tomatoes, skinned and deseeded
4 tablespoons shredded fresh basil
25g (1oz) butter
175g (6oz) chestnut mushrooms, sliced
1 tablespoon sun-dried tomatoes, cut into thin strips
salt and freshly ground black pepper.

TO GARNISH:
3 tablespoons freshly grated Parmesan cheese
3 tablespoons shredded fresh basil

Heat the oil and cook the onion, potatoes, fennel, carrots and garlic gently for 10 minutes in a covered saucepan, without colouring. Add the sun-dried tomato paste, red pepper, stock and tomatoes. Cover, bring to the boil and simmer gently for about 20-30 minutes until the vegetables are tender. Cool a little, then process to a coarse purée in a food processor or liquidiser. Add the shredded fresh basil.

Separately, melt the butter and sauté the mushrooms until they are crisp and brown. Add to the soup together with the strips of sun-dried tomatoes. Taste for seasoning. Serve with Parmesan cheese and lots of fresh basil.

New England Carrot, Apricot and Sesame Soup

The creator of this recipe, entered in our first 'Create a Soup' competition, is a retired French teacher and interpreter, Mrs Antoniades. She is a long-term homemade soup addict from London. As well as having appeared on an Open University programme called 'A Soup and a Sonnet', she regularly cooks soup for her family and friends. Married to a Cypriot, she has learned much about Middle Eastern cookery, hence the apricots that give this soup what Mrs Antoniades aptly describes as its 'sweet and sour allure'.

PREPARATION AND COOKING TIME: 1 hour
SERVES: 6

225g (8oz) dried apricots, soaked overnight in 1.2 litres (2 pints) water
1 medium onion, finely chopped
3 medium carrots, thinly sliced
1 cinnamon stick
1 bay leaf
570ml (1 pint) light chicken stock (see page 7)
Salt and freshly ground black pepper
150ml (¼ pint) Greek yoghurt
1 tablespoon clear honey

TO GARNISH:
1 tablespoon honey
2 tablespoons sesame seeds, toasted

Drain the apricots and set aside 570ml (1 pint) of the soaking liquor. Place the apricots, apricot liquor, onion, carrots, cinnamon, bay leaf, stock, salt and pepper in a saucepan. Cover, bring to the boil and simmer gently for 50 minutes, adding more water if necessary. Take out the cinnamon stick and bay leaf and skim off any fat. Cool a little, then purée in a liquidiser with the yoghurt. Taste for seasoning. Chill very well.

To toast the sesame seeds, heat a pan and when very hot add the seasame seeds. Shake over a moderate heat until the seeds begin to brown. Cool.

Serve the soup with a little honey drizzled over and a sprinkling of toasted seasame seeds.

Jewish Chicken Soup

Nikki Martin, our University of the South Bank placement student, gave us her grandmother Stella Richardson's recipe for 'Jewish penicillin', a restorative chicken broth which 'her mother' used to give her when she was ill. It is also traditionally eaten on Friday night, Shabbat, before roast chicken. The bones of this chicken are used to make the next week's soup. This soup is even better eaten the day after making and freezes especially well.

PREPARATION AND COOKING TIME : 2 hours 30 minutes
SERVES : 6

1 chicken, cut into 8 pieces, (and the giblets if
                included with the chicken) or chicken bones
3.15 litres (5½ pints) water
2 tablespoons chopped mixed fresh herbs
1 small leek, chopped
1 small swede, chopped
4 sticks celery, halved
1 large onion, coarsely chopped
450g (1lb) carrots, chopped
salt and freshly ground black pepper

TO GARNISH:
110g (4oz) shelled fresh green peas,
                or, if unavailable, frozen peas
110g (4oz) lochoen, available in specialist shops,
                or egg vermicelli

For the stock, put the chicken into a large saucepan with the water. Cover, bring to the boil and simmer very gently for 5 minutes, carefully skimming off any scum which forms on the surface. Add the chopped herbs and all the vegetables except the carrots. Simmer very gently for 1½ hours, skimming from time to time.

Remove the chicken with a slotted spoon and separate the meat from the bone, reserving it for the soup. Cover and simmer for a further 30 minutes. Discard the vegetables. Cool the stock and chill overnight. Remove the solid fat which will have formed on the surface.

Transfer the stock to a large saucepan, cover, bring to the boil and add the carrots. Taste for seasoning and simmer for 10-15 minutes until the carrots are tender. Meanwhile, cut the chicken into bite-sized pieces.

Add the peas and lochoen, or egg vermicelli, and cook for about 5 minutes. Return the chicken pieces to the soup. Serve.

Lentil and Tomato Soup with Cumin and Coriander

The story behind this soup is already quite well-known as it featured in one of our magazine advertisements. Inspired by Indian lentil dals, the soup company decided to create an Indian soup. The new recipe was first revealed at one of our regular employee soup tastings which Nina Bahd from our accounts department, who also just happens to have a diploma in five star catering, had attended. Nina did not approve of the efforts of our recipe developers and subsequently brought in a sample of her own family recipe. This turned out to be so delicious that we insisted on having the recipe. However as the recipe had been passed down through the generations from mother to daughter, Nina had never measured ingredients or written down the amounts - so we had to watch her cook it and make notes. Now it is a very popular flavour in our all-year-round range and has been given the seal of authenticity by Nina's husband, Jogeshwar.

PREPARATION AND COOKING TIME: 50 minutes
SERVES: 6

2 tablespoons extra virgin olive oil
1 medium onion, finely chopped
3/4 teaspoon ground coriander
3/4 teaspoon ground turmeric
3/4 teaspoon ground cumin
pinch of ground cloves
350 g (12oz) red lentils, washed
1.2 litres (2 pints) vegetable stock (see page 6)
400g (14oz) tinned chopped tomatoes
20g (3/4 oz) fresh coriander leaves
salt and freshly ground black pepper

TO GARNISH:
1 tablespoon extra virgin olive oil
1 large fresh green chilli, chopped
2 tablespoons fresh coriander leaves

Heat the oil and cook the onion for 5 minutes in a covered saucepan, without colouring. Add the dried spices and cook, stirring, for 5 minutes. Add the lentils and stock, cover and bring to the boil. Simmer gently for about 20 minutes until the lentils are tender. Add the tomatoes and simmer for 10 minutes. Cool a little, then purée in a liquidiser with the fresh coriander leaves. Taste for seasoning.

Heat the oil for the garnish and sauté the chopped fresh green chilli for 2 minutes over a moderate heat.

Serve the soup garnished with the sautéed chilli and fresh coriander leaves.

Moroccan Chicken and Lemon Soup

Heather Alway was born in New Zealand but raised on traditional British food. In her teens she discovered Chinese cuisine which she says was a 'Damascus Road experience' leading to a lifelong interest in international cookery.

In 1964, she and her husband spent three weeks touring the newly independent Morocco: 'meeting beautiful and kindly people in countryside alternately lush or barren and mountainous, gently tinted by mineral deposits – a vast watercolour landscape where all the senses combined to impact an unforgettable impression'. The food was also memorable and back in New Zealand she added extra stock, pickled lemon slices, spices and herbs to a leftover chicken casserole to try and recreate the flavour of a country she has never forgotten.

PREPARATION AND COOKING TIME: 1 hour 15 minutes
SERVES: 6

2 tablespoons each of sunflower oil and extra virgin olive oil
600g (1lb 5oz) chicken legs, jointed and skinned
2 small onions, roughly chopped
1 leek, cut into 1cm (½ in) slices
2 medium carrots, roughly chopped
3 sticks celery, cut into 1cm (½ in) slices
2 large garlic cloves, crushed
2 tablespoons honey
4 tablespoons raisins
3-4 teaspoons hot curry powder, to taste
1 teaspoon ground cumin
½ teaspoon ground allspice
1 litre (1¾ pints) chicken stock (see page 7)
50g (2oz) long grain rice
salt and freshly ground black pepper
1 large unwaxed lemon, thinly sliced

TO GARNISH:
150 ml (¼ pint) Greek yoghurt
2 tablespoons chopped fresh coriander

Heat the oils with ¼ teaspoon salt and brown the chicken pieces lightly on both sides. Remove the chicken. In the same covered saucepan, cook the onion gently until soft, without colouring. Add the leeks, carrots, celery and garlic and cook for 2 minutes. Stir in the honey, raisins, curry powder, cumin and allspice and stir over the heat for 1 minute.

Return the chicken pieces to the pan with the rice, lemon slices and raisins and stir to coat in the spices. Pour over the stock, stirring well, and bring to the boil. Cover and simmer gently for 20-25 minutes until the chicken is cooked, stirring occasionally. Remove the chicken meat from the bones and return to the pan. Taste for seasoning and serve garnished with a swirl of yoghurt and a sprinkling of fresh coriander.

Chicory Soup

This recipe was sent in to us by a man who grew chicory in his market garden and wanted to show what a good soup it would make. He was right about the soup - it's delicious - but we never did buy any of his chicory. The reason for this is lost, along with the grower's name, because this recipe was found in our huge scrapbox of cuttings. Anyway, thank you, whoever you are!

PREPARATION AND COOKING TIME: 1 hour
SERVES : 6

50g (2oz) butter
2 heads of chicory, sliced
1 medium onion, finely sliced
110g (4oz) parsnip, roughly chopped
400g (14oz) potato, peeled and sliced
570 ml (1 pint) vegetable stock (see page 6)
1 mace blade
1 bay leaf
lemon juice to taste
275 ml (½ pint) milk
150 ml (¼ pint) double cream
salt and freshly ground black pepper

TO GARNISH:
reserved chicory shreds
6 sprigs of fresh flat-leaf parsley

Melt the butter and cook the chicory, onion, parsnip and potatoes gently for 10 minutes, without colouring. Reserve a few shreds of chicory for the garnish. Add the stock, mace blade and bay leaf and bring to the boil. Simmer for 30 minutes. Remove the mace blade and bay leaf and purée in a liquidiser. Add the lemon juice, milk and cream and taste for seasoning.

Reheat and serve with the reserved chicory shreds and small sprigs of flat-leaf parsley.

Tomato and Tarragon Soup

If you love the distinctive flavour of tarragon, this is the soup for you. It may seem like an unusual combination but the addition of the herb adds sophistication to Britain's favourite flavour and elevates it to dinner party status.

PREPARATION AND COOKING TIME: 1 hour
SERVES: 6

40g (1½ oz) butter
1 tablespoon extra virgin olive oil
1 medium onion, finely chopped
1 stick celery, sliced
110g (4oz) carrot, sliced
1 garlic clove, chopped
675g (1½lb) fresh ripe tomatoes, skinned and chopped
  or 2 x 400g (14oz) tins chopped tomatoes
2 tablespoons tomato purée
1 bay leaf
1-2 tablespoons chopped fresh tarragon
1 litre (1¾ pints) light chicken stock (see page 7)
1-2 teaspoons sugar, or to taste
1 small strip lemon rind
salt and freshly ground black pepper

TO GARNISH:
freshly ground black pepper

Melt the butter and oil together in a large saucepan and cook the vegetables and garlic for 2 minutes, without colouring. Add the tomatoes, tomato purée, bay leaf, tarragon, chicken stock, sugar and lemon rind. Simmer gently, uncovered, for 20 minutes. Discard the strip of lemon rind and bay leaf, and then purée in a liquidiser. Pass through a fine sieve into a clean saucepan. Taste for seasoning and reheat. Serve with a twist of black pepper over each bowl.

Real Dutch Pea Soup

This recipe has been passed down through Emma Collins' family for years. She remembers eating 'Real Dutch Pea Soup' prepared by her grandmother, when she was young. Generations of use have honed this recipe to a state of absolute perfection!

PREPARATION AND COOKING TIME: 3 hours 10 minutes
SERVES: 6 generously

450g (1lb) green split peas, washed
450g (1lb) shin of beef
soup bone, if available
450g (1lb) potatoes, peeled and roughly chopped
3 litres (5 pints) water
700g (1½ lb) leeks, finely sliced
1 medium celeriac, peeled and cut into 4cm (1½ in) sticks
salt and freshly ground black pepper

TO GARNISH:
3 tablespoons chopped fresh celery leaves

Soak the green split peas overnight in plenty of water. Drain and put into a large saucepan with the beef soup bone, potatoes and water. Cover, bring to the boil, skim off any scum and simmer gently for at least 2 hours. Remove the beef and tear into small pieces. Squash the vegetables against the side of the pan with a wooden spoon. Return the meat to the pan along with the leeks and celeriac. Taste for seasoning. Cover and simmer for 1 hour. Remove the soup bone and serve hot garnished with celery leaves.

Lentil and Lemon Soup

I don't think anybody asked Anna Abrahams, the newest member of our sales department, if she liked soup when she came for her interview. Once she had got the job, however, we soon found out she was just as passionate about soup as the rest of us – in fact she makes it every day! This creation of hers is refreshing and substantial at the same time. Anna is a vegetarian and this meal-in-a-soup, packed full of pulses, is full of diet-enriching protein. It's also fine for vegans and those allergic to dairy produce.

PREPARATION AND COOKING TIME: 40 minutes
SERVES: 6

2 tablespoons extra virgin olive oil
1 large onion, finely chopped
1 garlic clove, crushed
150g (5oz) red lentils, washed
570ml (1 pint) vegetable stock (see page 6)
1 x 400g (14oz) tin chopped tomatoes
2 teaspoons tomato purée
2 tablespoons finely chopped fresh thyme
salt and freshly ground black pepper
juice of ½ lemon, or to taste

TO GARNISH:
6 small sprigs fresh thyme

Heat the oil and cook the onion and garlic gently for 10 minutes without colouring. Add the lentils and stir to coat well in the oil. Add the stock and bring to the boil. Skim off any scum. Add the tinned tomatoes, tomato purée and three-quarters of the thyme. Bring back to the boil and simmer, covered for 15-20 minutes, stirring occasionally. Taste for seasoning and add the remaining chopped fresh thyme. Add the lemon juice little by little to taste. Serve garnished with sprigs of thyme.

CHAPTER FOUR

Fancy

'The great fashion is to place four fine
soups at the four corners with four dish
stands between each two, with four salt
cellars placed near the soup tureen'

Nicolas de Bonnefors, Delices de la Campagne 1652
Describing a banquet in the reign of Louis XIV

Fresh Salmon, Tomato and Basil Soup

As Scotland is famous for its soup making, it seemed appropriate that we should have a soup inspired by that country on the market. We therefore held a competition in the Scotland on Sunday newspaper to find a new soup using the finest of Scottish ingredients. This is the winning soup, using both fresh and smoked salmon. Its originator, Rita Brown owns the Hazelton Guesthouse with her husband Alan in Crail, Fife. Amazingly, Rita is completely self-taught and devises all her own recipes to serve to her guests. She believes in using only fresh and mostly local ingredients depending on the season and grows many of them herself. We couldn't agree more!

PREPARATION AND COOKING TIME: 45 minutes
SERVES : 6

25g (1oz) butter
1 medium onion, finely chopped
3 garlic cloves, crushed
3/4 teaspoon plain flour
900ml (1½ pints) fish stock (see page 8)
300ml (10½ floz) dry white wine
2 teaspoons tomato purée
¼ teaspoon cayenne pepper, or to taste
1 large bay leaf
450ml (3/4 pint) milk
200g (7oz) fresh salmon, skinned and any bones removed, cut into 2cm (3/4 in) dice
75g (3oz) smoked salmon trimmings, cut into small pieces
700g (1½ lb) ripe but firm tomatoes, skinned, deseeded and cut into 2cm (3/4 in) dice
1 tablespoon chopped fresh basil
salt and freshly ground black pepper

TO GARNISH:
150ml (¼ pint) single cream
6 small sprigs fresh basil
paprika

Heat the butter and cook the onion and garlic gently for 5 minutes in a covered saucepan, without colouring. Stir in the flour and cook for 2 minutes, stirring constantly. Gradually add the stock, white wine, tomato purée, cayenne and bay leaf. Cover, bring to the boil and simmer gently for 10 minutes until the onions are soft. Cool a little, then remove the bay leaf and purée the soup in a liquidiser. Return to a clean saucepan and reheat gently. When the soup is very hot, add the salmon, smoked salmon, tomatoes and basil. Simmer gently for 2 minutes until the salmon is just firm. Taste for seasoning, taking care as smoked salmon is quite salty. Serve garnished with a swirl of cream, the basil sprigs and a dusting of paprika.

Cream of Chicken Soup with Lemon and Tarragon

This was the first meat soup introduced by the soup company. Later when we decided, for variety's sake, to replace it with something else, we got a deluge of letters calling for its reinstatement. As a result it was brought back for a few years but now it has gone again so fans must resort to making it themselves.

PREPARATION AND COOKING TIME: 1 hour
SERVES: 6

40g (1½ oz) butter
1 medium onion, finely chopped
110g (4 oz) chicken breast meat, cut into small pieces
2 teaspoons dried tarragon
25g (1oz) plain flour
570ml (1 pint) vegetable stock (see page 6)
grated rind and juice of 1 lemon
2 teaspoons soy sauce
150 ml (¼ pint) single cream
salt and freshly ground black pepper

Melt the butter and cook the onion in a covered saucepan for 15–20 minutes. Add the chicken pieces and tarragon and cook for 5 minutes. Stir in the flour and cook for 1 minute. Gradually add the stock, lemon rind, lemon juice and soy sauce, cover and cook until the chicken is tender. Stir in the cream. There is a chance that the soup may curdle a little at this stage. Don't be put off by this as the soup is delicious. Reheat gently without boiling, season and serve.

Fresh Lobster and Leek Soup
or
Brot Giomach ùr Agus Leigis

Theona Morrison, a business counsellor and crofter, lives with her husband on the three mile long island of Grimsay situated just off the island of North Uist in the Outer Hebrides of Scotland. Grimsay has traditionally been, and continues to be, a Gaelic speaking crofting and fishing community. The Morrison's croft is surrounded on three sides by the sea and Theona's husband has spent a lifetime fishing for lobsters along the Atlantic coasts of the Uists. Most Grimsay crofters are able to provide a lot of their own food - mostly fine shellfish, hardy vegetables that can survive the weather and the meat of the rare black, four-horned Hebridean sheep which have been re-introduced to the island. Theona often has visitors from far afield and likes to offer them as much local produce as possible. It was with this in mind that she created this soup. She says: ' I hope you enjoy this taste of the Uists - Slàinte mhath agus sonas - good health and happiness'.

PREPARATION AND COOKING TIME: 1 hour
SERVES: 6

> 2 cooked lobsters, each weighing 700g (1½lb)
> 1 bay leaf
> pinch of salt
> 50g (2oz) butter
> 2 small onions, finely chopped
> 1 large leek, chopped
> 1 medium carrot, chopped
> 4 medium potatoes, about 600g (1lb 5oz), peeled and chopped
> 275ml (½ pint) milk
> 1 glass of dry white wine
> juice of ½ lemon
> salt and freshly ground black pepper
> 150ml (¼ pint) single cream

TO GARNISH:
2 tablespoons finely chopped fresh flat-leaf parsley

Throughly clean the lobster shells. Remove all the meat and cut into small pieces. Put all the bones into a saucepan with the bay leaf, pinch of salt and 1.5 litres (2¾ pints) water. Bring to the boil and simmer for 45 minutes, skimming from time to time. Strain well and reserve.

Melt the butter and cook the onion gently for a few minutes in a covered saucepan, without colouring. Add the leek, carrots and potatoes and cook for 10 minutes until soft.

Add 1.2 litres (2 pints) reserved stock to the vegetables, cover and simmer for a further 20 minutes until the vegetables are tender. Purée the soup with the milk in a liquidiser. Return to a clean saucepan and stir in the lobster meat, white wine and lemon juice. Taste for seasoning. Reheat gently and stir in the cream just before serving. Garnish with chopped parsley.

Lamb Tagine

William Kendall, the soup company's MD, comes from a farming family and still helps to run the family farm and his wife's farm in Suffolk. He also grows his own vegetables, distills his own fruit cordials, shoots, hunts, fishes and cooks. Here is one of his favourite stew/soups which is a perfect dinner party dish for people with limited time available!

PREPARATION AND COOKING TIME: 1 hour
SERVES: 6

2 tablespoons extra virgin olive oil
700g (1½lb) boned shoulder of lamb, cut into small slivers
2 medium onions, finely chopped
2 medium carrots, roughly chopped
1 large stick celery, roughly chopped
2 garlic cloves, crushed
2 large teaspoons plain flour
1.2 litres (2 pints) vegetable stock (see page 6)
1½ teaspoons harissa, or to taste
    or, if unavailable, use 1 tablespoon paprika and
    ½ teaspoon cayenne moistened with ½ tablespoon
    extra virgin olive oil
2 tablespoons fresh coriander leaves
    or 1 teaspoon coriander seeds, crushed
1 teaspoon cumin seeds
Salt

TO GARNISH:
3 tablespoons fresh coriander leaves

Heat the oil and brown the lamb. Remove from the pan, then, in the same pan, sauté the onions, carrots, celery and garlic until golden. Stir in the flour and cook for 2 minutes, stirring. Gradually stir in the stock, return the meat to the vegetables and add the harissa or paprika and cayenne mixture. Add the coriander leaves, or crushed coriander seeds, and the cumin seeds. Cover, bring to the boil and simmer very gently for about 1 hour. Add more stock if necessary. Add salt to taste and serve garnished with fresh coriander leaves.

Venison Soup

This recipe was developed by our recipe testers but as yet, has not been launched. We wanted to do a rich, dark gamey special occasion soup and this is the result, enriched with mushrooms, tarragon and red wine. Always on the hunt for the best ingredients, we looked at using wild venison which has the best flavour and is also low in fat but the cost for the quantities we need was prohibitive. This, obviously, is no excuse for the home cook, so give it a try!

PREPARATION AND COOKING TIME: 1 hour 15 minutes
SERVES: 6

40g (1½oz) butter
2 medium onions, finely chopped
1 garlic clove, crushed
125g (4½oz) chestnut mushrooms, sliced
200g (7oz) venison, cut into small strips
1 dessertspoon plain flour
2 tablespoons tomato purée
1 dessertspoon chopped fresh tarragon
1 litre (1¾ pints) game stock (see page 10)
110ml (4 floz) red wine
Salt and freshly ground black pepper

TO GARNISH:
1 tablespoon sunflower oil
3 rashers unsmoked streaky bacon, chopped
  or 1 small parsnip, shredded

Melt the butter and cook the onion and garlic gently for 5 minutes in a covered saucepan, without colouring. Add the mushrooms and venison and stir to seal the meat for 2 minutes. Stir in the flour, tomato purée and tarragon, then add the stock and red wine. Cover, bring to the boil and simmer gently for about 45 minutes until the meat is tender. Taste for seasoning.

Meanwhile heat the oil for the garnish and sauté the bacon or parsnips over a moderate heat until crisp. Drain on kitchen paper.

Serve the soup garnished with crisp bacon or parsnip.

Lamb and Rowan Soup with Ale

A finalist in our Scottish Soup Competition, which we ran in the Scotland on Sunday newspaper, Teresa Maley's soup started as a lighter version of a favourite family dish: Lamb Sam (Lamb fillets and onions cooked in Sam Smith's lager). Teresa likes to try combinations of real ales in meat soups as their distinctive flavours produce very interesting results. In Selkirk where she lives, Teresa says that 'comfort foods are needed almost all year round!!'

PREPARATION AND COOKING TIME: 1 hour 10 minutes
SERVES: 6

FOR THE STOCK:
570ml (1 pint) chicken or vegetable stock (see page 7 & 6)
1 small bottle Traquair Ale, or, if unavailable, any strong Scottish ale
1 bay leaf
1 garlic clove
6-8 juniper berries
6 whole shallots

1 tablespoon extra virgin olive oil
1 large red onion, finely chopped
2 rashers smoked streaky bacon, finely diced
2 teaspoons brown sugar
225g (8oz) boned leg of lamb,
  cut into 4cm (1 (1½in) slivers
20g (3/4 oz) rolled oats
570ml (1 pint) stock (see below)
2 dessertspoons rowan jelly or, if unavailable,
  seedless bramble conserve
whites of 2 large leeks, shredded
salt and freshly ground black pepper

TO GARNISH:
DUMPLINGS MADE WITH:
50g (2oz) self raising flour
25g (1oz) shredded suet
grated rind of ¼ lemon
¼ level teaspoon salt
water

For the stock, put the stock ingredients into a saucepan, bring to the boil and simmer until the liquid has reduced to 570ml (1 pint). Strain.

Heat the oil and cook the onion and bacon over a moderate heat, sprinkled with brown sugar, until they begin to brown. Add the lamb slivers and cook until brown. Throw in the oats and add the stock and rowan jelly. Cover, bring to the boil and simmer for 20-30 minutes until the lamb is tender.

For the dumplings, mix the dumpling ingredients with enough water to make a soft dough. Shape with floured hands into 12 dumplings.

Add the leeks to the soup and settle the dumplings on the surface of the soup. Cover and simmer for about 10 minutes until the leeks are just soft and the dumplings risen and cooked. Taste for seasoning. Serve, giving 2 dumplings to each guest.

Cream of Fennel Soup

On a visit to our publishers, Boxtree, while browsing through their recent cookery publications, I came across Marimar Torres' Catalan Country Kitchen. Out of curiosity, I photocopied a page of soup recipes and circled the one I wanted to be tested. The recipe tester cooked the wrong one but it was very good - so here it is.

PREPARATION AND COOKING TIME: 1 hour 20 minutes
SERVES: 6

50g (2oz) butter
2 medium onions, finely chopped
1 garlic clove, finely chopped
2 heads of fennel, about 450g (1lb), finely sliced
900ml (1½ pints) light chicken stock (see page 7),
        or 1.2 litres (2 pints) if serving chilled
finely grated rind of ½ orange
110ml (4floz) double cream, or yoghurt if serving chilled
salt and freshly ground black pepper

Melt the butter and cook the onion and garlic gently for 10 minutes in a covered saucepan, without colouring. Add the fennel, cover and cook gently for 30 minutes to bring out the full flavour of the fennel. Stir from time to time. Add the chicken stock and orange rind. Cover, bring to the boil and simmer gently for about 30 minutes until the vegetables are tender. Cool a little, then purée in a liquidiser and pass through a sieve. Stir in the cream and taste for seasoning. Reheat gently. The soup is delicious served either hot or chilled.

From Catalan Country Kitchen, Marimar Torres, Boxtree 1995

Clam Chowder

Interior designer Emma Farquarson's love for Clam Chowder started at a very young age and stems from staying with her cousins in America. After leaving school, she went to work at the Sconset Café on Nantucket Island where she learnt to make this delicious soup herself. The following recipe is the result of many refinements over the years.

PREPARATION AND COOKING TIME : 1 hour 10 minutes
SERVES: 6

3 medium potatoes, about 700g (1½ lb), peeled and quartered
1.35 Kg (3lb) baby clams in their shells
1 tablespoon sunflower oil
175g (6oz) unsmoked streaky bacon, finely chopped
1 medium onion, very finely chopped
3 sticks celery, very finely chopped
2 teaspoons chopped fresh thyme
1 level tablespoon dried dill weed
½ teaspoon ground white pepper
25g (1oz) plain flour
570ml (1pint) fish stock (see page 8)
150ml (¼ pint) dry white wine
3 bay leaves
275 ml (½ pint) double cream

TO GARNISH:
reserved clams in their shells
2 tablespoons finely chopped fresh flat-leaf parsley

Simmer the potatoes in plenty of salted water until tender. Cool and slice.

Wash the clams at least 6 times in plenty of cold water to remove any grit. Put them into a large saucepan, cover and place over a high heat. Cook until the clams are just open, shaking the pan frequently. Cool. Remove all but 18 clams from their shells, reserving the 18 for the garnish. Also reserve the pan juices.

Fry the bacon over a medium heat until crisp. Add the onion and celery. Cover and cook gently for 8 minutes. Add the thyme, dill weed and pepper and cook for 2 minutes. Stir in the flour and cook very gently, stirring constantly, for 5 minutes.

Put the clam juices, fish stock, white wine and bay leaves in a separate pan. Bring to the boil and simmer gently for 5 minutes. Gradually stir the broth into the vegetable mixture, cover and simmer gently for 10 minutes, stirring frequently. Add the potatoes, roughly mashing one quarter of the potatoes against the side of the pan, then add the clams.

Gently reheat the chowder, stir in the cream and garnish with the reserved clams and finely chopped parsley.

Crab Bisque

In a bisque, the shell of the featured creature is ground up to give the soup substance and flavour. Fresh crab is far superior to all the other forms that it is sold in, because the shell can produce a stock that is far more delicious than the crab meat within. A fresh crab makes a good cheap informal meal, but when made into a soup, it becomes elevated to gourmet status.

PREPARATION AND COOKING TIME: 2 hours 15 minutes
SERVES: 6

2 large cooked crabs
110g (4oz) butter
1 medium onion, finely chopped
1 medium carrot, finely chopped
2 medium sticks celery, finely chopped
4 garlic cloves, crushed
1 small bunch of fresh tarragon or parsley, chopped
1 bay leaf
3 sprigs of fresh thyme
a few fresh parsley stalks
110g (4oz) tomato purée
a pinch of chilli powder to taste
150 ml (¼ pint) dry white wine
150 ml (¼ pint) brandy
1.5 litres (2½ pints) water
75g (3oz) plain flour
275 ml (½ pint) double cream
salt and freshly ground black pepper

TO GARNISH:
3 tablespoons hot croûtons (see page 108 but do not toss in Parmesan cheese)

Remove the meat from the crab, roughly chop and reserve. Crush the shell and claws into small pieces using a rolling pin.

Heat 25g (1oz) butter and cook the onion, carrot, celery, garlic, tarragon, bay leaf, thyme sprigs and parsley stalks gently until soft in a covered saucepan, without colouring. Stir in the tomato purée, chilli powder and the crushed shell, wine and brandy. Pour in the water, cover, bring to the boil and simmer for 40 minutes with the lid ajar. Strain well.

Melt the remaining butter in a clean saucepan and stir in the flour. Gradually stir in the strained liquor, add the reserved meat and, continuing to stir, bring to the boil and simmer for 2 minutes. Stir in the cream and season well. Reheat and serve offering hot croûtons to your guests.

Celery and Lemon Vichyssoise with Prawns

This soup has a wonderful sounding name – classic with a twist. Retired teacher Jean Smith created it for our 1995 Good Housekeeping 'Create a Soup' competition because she finds basic Vichyssoise rather dull. Using it as a base, she added a clever combination of ingredients which taste as though they were made for each other. Unsurprisingly, she has already won numerous cookery competitions.

PREPARATION AND COOKING TIME: 45 minutes
SERVES: 6

10g (½oz) butter
1 small onion, finely sliced
350g (12oz) celery, cut into 1cm (½ in) slices
225g (8oz) white of leek, sliced
450g (1lb) potatoes, peeled and sliced
2 strips of lemon rind
seeds from 5 cardamon pods, crushed
¼ teaspoon celery salt
¼ teaspoon sugar
900ml (1½ pints) chicken stock (see page 7)
150ml (¼ pint) single cream
salt and freshly ground black pepper
lemon juice, to taste
110g (4oz) cooked peeled prawns, roughly chopped

TO GARNISH:
slivers of lemon
sprigs of dill or fennel
    or 2 teaspoons finely chopped
    fresh flat-leaf parsley

Melt the butter and cook the onion, celery, leek and potatoes gently for 5 minutes in a covered saucepan, without colouring. Stir in the lemon rind, cardamon seeds, celery salt, sugar and stock. Cover, bring to the boil and simmer gently for about 30 minutes until the vegetables are tender. Cool a little, remove the lemon rind, then purée in a liquidiser and pass through a sieve. Stir in the cream and season with salt, pepper and lemon juice. Add the prawns and reheat gently without boiling. The soup is delicious hot or chilled, garnished with slivers of lemon and sprigs of dill or fennel, or with pinches of chopped fresh parsley.

Sorrel and Oyster Soup

When Caroline Jeremy was doing her 'stage' (a French cook's apprenticeship) at Paris's most famous restaurant La Tour D'Argent, she had dinner with the head chef. In no time at all, he produced an incredible meal - very simple and full of flavour. Here is an approximation of his soup recipe - the lemony sorrel and the fresh salty oysters complement each other perfectly.

PREPARATION AND COOKING TIME: 20 minutes
SERVES : 6

1.75 litres (3 pints) fish stock (see page 8)
salt and freshly ground black pepper
12 fresh oysters, removed from their shells
225g (8oz) fresh sorrel leaves, finely shredded

TO GARNISH:
150ml (¼ pint) single cream

Put the stock into a large saucepan, cover and bring to the boil. Taste for seasoning. Add the oysters and cook for 1 minute. Distribute the sorrel between the soup bowls and ladle over the broth and oysters. Serve immediately with a drizzle of cream.

CHAPTER FIVE

Plain

Economical Soup

Take one bean (Haricot or Butter), 7 pints of water, simmer
for three weeks; then take out the bean and season to taste.
If thick soup is preferred, leave the bean in.

Miss Rayner, St Helens (from a wartime recipe book)

Spinach with Nutmeg Soup

This was the fourth product to be produced by the New Covent Garden Soup Company and is still one of our most popular. However, when we were testing it, many said that the colour - a dark, murky green - would put people off. We were adamant that this was a natural homemade colour and that our customers would appreciate this - the first of many times that we have defied an established 'food industry' belief and laid it to rest. Here, despite suffering from slight 'ennui' when it comes to eating our soups at home, we never tire of this one because of its simple, fresh flavour.

PREPARATION AND COOKING TIME: 30 minutes
SERVES: 6

25g (1oz) butter
1 large onion, finely chopped
25g (1oz) plain flour
900ml (1½ pints) vegetable stock (see page 6)
juice of ½ lemon to taste
700g (1½ lb) fresh spinach
freshly grated nutmeg
150ml (¼ pint) milk
50ml (2floz) single cream
Salt and freshly ground black pepper

TO GARNISH:
2 tablespoons chopped fresh herbs
150ml (¼ pint) single cream

Melt the butter and cook the onion very gently for 10 minutes in a covered saucepan, without colouring. Stir in the flour and cook gently for 2 minutes. Gradually add the stock, lemon juice, spinach and nutmeg. Cover, bring to the boil and simmer for about 5 minutes until the spinach has wilted. Cool a little, then purée in a liquidiser. Return to a clean saucepan and stir in the milk and cream. Taste for seasoning. Reheat gently and serve garnished with chopped fresh herbs and a swirl of cream.

Celery and Potato Soup with Cheese

Perfectly simple to make and perfectly delicious to eat, this soup is the creation of Jo Gilks, our Recipe Tester. Jo used to be a city banker but decided that her real interest lay in food and she is now a high-quality caterer and home economist. In 1992 Jo assisted Antonio Carluccio on the BBC's 'Hot Chefs' and more recently, she has worked on the book 'A Passion for Italy' for his television series. For our book, Jo has patiently tested over 150 soup recipes, remaining enthusiastic throughout.

PREPARATION AND COOKING TIME: 1 hour 15 minutes
SERVES: 6

50g (2oz) butter
1 medium onion, finely chopped
1 large leafy head of celery, finely chopped
450g (1lb) potatoes, peeled and sliced
725ml (1¼ pint) light chicken stock (see page 7)
150ml (¼ pint) double cream
salt and freshly ground pepper

TO GARNISH:
50g (2oz) mature Cheddar cheese, grated

Melt the butter in a large saucepan. Add the onion, celery and potatoes and cook gently, covered, for 10 minutes, without colouring. Add the stock and season well. Cover, bring to the boil and simmer gently for about 30 minutes until the vegetables are tender. Cool a little and then process half the soup finely and half the soup coarsely in a food processor. Return the soup to the pan, stir in the cream and taste for seasoning. Reheat gently and serve piping hot sprinkled with grated cheese.

Ratatouille Soup

This soup version of the French vegetable casserole was invented by Sarah Randell, who works in our Recipe Development Department. Sarah, who was trained at Leith's School of food and wine and has worked at Quaglino's, was inspired by wonderful rustic ratatouille eaten alfresco in the South of France.

PREPARATION AND COOKING TIME : 30 minutes
SERVES : 6

1 tablespoon extra virgin olive oil
1 large onion, finely chopped
1 garlic clove, crushed
100g (3½ oz) aubergine, cut into 2.5cm (1in) dice
125g (4½ oz) courgette, cut into 2.5cm (1in) dice
60g (2½ oz) green pepper, cut into 2.5cm (1in) dice
60g (2½ oz) red pepper, cut into 2.5cm (1in) dice
110g (4 oz) fresh plum tomatoes, roughly chopped
3 tablespoons tomato purée
1 teaspoon brown sugar
pinch of cayenne pepper
900ml (1½ pints) vegetable stock (see page 6)
20g (¾ oz) sun-dried tomatoes, diced
salt and freshly ground black pepper

TO GARNISH :
a handful of fresh basil leaves

Heat the oil and cook the onion gently for 10 minutes in a covered saucepan, without colouring. Add the garlic, 40g (1½ oz) aubergine, 75g (3oz) courgettes, 25g (1oz) each of green and red pepper, the tomatoes, tomato purée, brown sugar, cayenne and stock. Cover, bring to the boil and simmer for 10 minutes over a medium heat. Purée the soup in a liquidiser and pour into a clean saucepan.

Fill a saucepan with salted water and bring to the boil. Add the remaining vegetables and simmer for 1 minute, drain and then add to the soup along with the sun-dried tomatoes. This soup is delicious hot or chilled. Serve garnished with fresh basil leaves.

Mrs Kendall's Lentil Soup

Mrs Kendall, mother of our Managing Director, writes: 'Long before son William began his soup job, my annual Christmas Eve cheese, wine and soup party was a very well attended local event for fifty friends and family. Soup served in mugs from a large stewpot on a trolley is always in huge demand and is still thought possibly a little better than that made by the soup company.' Our Lentil with Winter Vegetable Soup is made with vegetable stock but Mrs Kendall's soup uses gammon stock which gives it a rich, deep flavour – we leave it for you to decide.

PREPARATION AND COOKING TIME : 3 hours 30 minutes
SERVES : 6

2 medium onions, finely chopped
250g (9oz) carrots, finely chopped
110g (4oz) red lentils
1.7 litres (3 pints) gammon stock (see below)
fresh ground black pepper

FOR THE STOCK:
This is an ideal way of using the stock
from the cooking of a 2.8Kg (7lb) gammon with
2 tablespoons brown sugar, 2 tablespoons malt vinegar,
1 bay leaf and water to cover

TO GARNISH:
2 tablespoons finely chopped fresh flat-leaf parsley

Put the soup ingredients into a saucepan, cover, bring to the boil and simmer for about 30 minutes until the vegetables and lentils are tender. Cool a little, then purée in a liquidiser.

Reheat and serve garnished with chopped fresh parsley.

Mangetout Soup

Mary Rayner, a children's book author and illustrator from Wiltshire, finds that soup-making is the ideal way to unwind from the intense concentration that her work requires. For this recipe, she thought that it would be nice to make a pea soup with the fresh taste of the green pods. Its beautiful green colour must appeal to her illustrator's eye.

PREPARATION AND COOKING TIME: 40 minutes
SERVES: 6

25g (1oz) butter
1 large onion, finely chopped
110g (4oz) yellow split peas, soaked for 1 hour
in plenty of water
900 ml (1½ pints) vegetable stock (see page 6)
250g (9oz) mangetout
salt and freshly ground black pepper

Melt the butter and cook the onion gently for 5 minutes in a covered saucepan, without colouring. Add the split peas and stir to coat in the butter. Add the stock, cover, bring to the boil and simmer for 30 minutes until tender. The time will vary according to the age and hardness of your split peas. Add the mangetout and continue to simmer for 5 minutes. Cool a little, then purée in a liquidiser. Taste for seasoning. Reheat just before serving.

White Bean, Tomato and Sage Soup

This combination of flavours originates from Italian peasant cooking and is a favourite of Caroline Jeremy who often makes this soup at home. However, when we try to make it in large quantities in our factory we have real problems: the beans must be soaked before cooking but each batch of beans seems to absorb a different amount of water making the soup's texture either too thin or too thick. Starch in the beans makes the thicker batches solidify in the carton so the soup comes out in a lump – not very palatable – although it's fine once it's heated up. So, because we won't be making it again, you should try it yourself – it really is worth it.

PREPARATION AND COOKING TIME: 1 hour 15 minutes
SERVES: 6

150g (5oz) dried butter beans   * (see soaking
60g (2½oz) dried haricot beans   instructions below)
25g (1oz) butter
½ medium onion, finely chopped
1 garlic clove, crushed
1.2 litres (2 pints) vegetable stock (see page 6)
1 heaped teaspoon tomato purée
150g (5oz) tinned chopped tomatoes
1 teaspoon demerara sugar
1 tablespoon finely chopped fresh sage
salt
150ml (¼ pint) milk
1 tablespoon double cream

* Soak the butter beans in 200ml (7fl oz) water for 1 hour.
* Soak the haricot beans in 75ml (3fl oz) water for 1 hour.

Melt the butter and cook the onion and garlic gently until soft in a covered saucepan, without colouring. Add the stock, tomato purée, butter beans and tomatoes. Cover, bring to the boil and simmer gently until the butter bean are tender. Cool a little, then purée in a liquidiser. Return to a clean saucepan and add the haricot beans, sugar, sage and salt to taste. Add more water if necessary to achieve the desired consistency. Simmer for about 45 minutes until the haricot beans are tender. Cool and stir in the milk and cream.

(V)

Jason Stead's Courgette and Brie Soup

Jason Stead is twelve years old and a pupil at Comberton Village College near Cambridge. He is a very keen cook and for a home economics assessment he had to prepare a mainly vegetable meal to serve four people. Remembering a vegetable soup with Brie in it that his mum's friend had made when he stayed in Scotland, he created his own version using courgettes, potatoes and onions. After practising at home, he made the soup for his teacher and served it with crusty bread - she loved it and gave Jason an A! The recipe came to the soup company via a home economist called Helen Kinton who works for Radio 2. She met Jason's father Mike, a manager for Anglian Windows, when she was having her conservatory built. He told her that his son had created a soup recipe and on tasting it, she thought it was good enough to feature on 'Helen Kinton with Mo's Munchies; Weekend Early Show, BBC Radio 2'. How did we meet Helen Kinton? Well, that's another story.....

PREPARATION AND COOKING TIME : 30 minutes
SERVES : 6

450g (1lb) courgettes, sliced
2 medium potatoes, about 350g (12oz), peeled and chopped
1 onion, finely chopped
1.2 litres (2 pints) vegetable stock (see page 6)
225g (8oz) Somerset Brie, remove end rind
        and cut into pieces
salt and freshly ground black pepper

Put all the ingredients except the Brie in a large saucepan. Cover, bring to the boil and simmer gently for about 15 minutes until the vegetables are tender. Stir in the cheese until melted. Cool a little, then purée in a liquidiser. Taste for seasoning.

Mushroom Soup with Parsley and Garlic

A simple but classic Mushroom soup that is loved by everyone. This is one of the first recipes ever created by Caroline Jeremy, now our Marketing Director, in the kitchen of her flat when she was working as a freelance recipe developer for the soup company back at the very beginning in 1987. The recipe was actually poached by Caroline from an old boyfriend who was obsessed with cooking. They eventually split up because he would not let her near the stove.

PREPARATION AND COOKING TIME: 40 minutes
SERVES: 6

25g (1oz) butter
½ medium onion, finely chopped
1 garlic clove, finely chopped
40g (1½ oz) plain flour
700ml (1¼ pints) vegetable stock (see page 6)
250g (9oz) chestnut mushrooms, sliced
1 tablespoon finely chopped fresh flat-leaf parsley
75ml (3 floz) single cream
Salt and freshly ground black pepper

TO GARNISH:
2 tablespoons finely chopped fresh flat-leaf parsley

Melt half the butter and cook the onion and garlic gently for 5 minutes in a covered saucepan, without colouring. Stir in the flour and cook gently for 1 minute, stirring. Gradually add the stock, stirring all the time. Add half the mushrooms and parsley. Cover, bring to the boil and simmer gently for about 10-15 minutes until the vegetables are tender. Cool a little, then purée in a liquidiser.

In the remaining butter, sauté the remaining mushrooms for 5 minutes until they begin to brown, then add to the puréed soup. Simmer gently for 3 minutes. Stir in the cream and taste for seasoning. Serve garnished with chopped fresh parsley.

Split Pea and Leek Soup

This soup originates in a Scottish Bank where the mother of Simon Bell, the soup company's Sales Director, works. At the Bank of Scotland in Dunfermline, an illicit trade is going on...... in recipes! Jenny Bell got her hands on this gem during one of these sessions and it has become her favourite. We're not going to reveal what we had to give to get it - but it was worth it.

PREPARATION AND COOKING TIME: 1 hour
SERVES: 6

60g (2½oz) butter
1 medium onion, finely chopped
2 large leeks, finely sliced, about 225g (8oz)
2 medium potatoes, about 350g (12oz), peeled and roughly chopped
110g (4oz) green split peas, soaked overnight in plenty of water
1.2 litres (2 pints) light chicken stock (see page 7)
salt and freshly ground black pepper

Melt the butter and cook the onion and leeks gently until soft in a covered saucepan, without colouring. Stir in the potatoes, green split peas and stock. Cover, bring to the boil and simmer gently for about 40 minutes until the split peas are tender. Cool a little, then purée in a liquidiser. Taste for seasoning. Reheat gently and serve.

Tuscan Bean Soup

There are thousands of bean soups in Tuscany- every Italian 'madre' has her own version of this wonderful peasant recipe using cannellini (small haricot beans). Inspired by these and the popularity of Tuscany as a holiday destination, we created our own version which is one of our most popular soups in cartons.

PREPARATION AND COOKING TIME: 2 hours
SERVES: 6

275g (10oz) mixed dried beans, washed, including chickpeas,
     soya, black-eyed, pinto, haricot and kidney beans
1 tablespoon extra virgin olive oil
1 large onion, chopped
1 small leek, sliced
4 garlic cloves, crushed
275ml (½ pint) vegetable stock (see page 6)
900 ml (1½ pints) water
460g (14oz) tinned chopped plum tomatoes
20g (¾ oz) finely chopped fresh flat-leaf parsley
75g (3oz) mushrooms, sliced
75g (3oz) shelled fresh green peas,
     or, if unavailable, frozen peas
1 teaspoon chopped fresh oregano
Salt and freshly ground black pepper

Soak the beans in plenty of cold water overnight. Drain and place in a saucepan with plenty of water. Bring to the boil and simmer gently for about 1 hour until the beans are tender. Drain.

Heat the oil and cook the onion, leek and garlic gently until soft in a covered saucepan, without colouring. Add the stock, water and cooked drained beans. Cover, bring to the boil and simmer for about 15 minutes. Add the tomatoes, parsley, mushrooms, peas and oregano, cover and simmer for a further 15 minutes until the vegetables and beans are tender. Cool a little, then purée one-quarter of the soup in a liquidiser. Return to the soup in the saucepan, taste for seasoning and simmer for 10 minutes. Serve. This soup is even more delicious if eaten the day after cooking.

Mrs MacKay's Scotch Broth

Stewart MacKay, a stalwart of the soup company since its earliest beginnings, has done every job going including chopping the vegetables, running the factory and supervising despatch. Currently he is a manager in our Sales Department and also runs his own company, Eventus, which runs our tasting stands at shows and exhibitions around the country. Stewart, like many others who work for the soup company, has roots in that land of soup lovers, Scotland. Consequently, he has a Scottish grandmother and all Scottish grandmothers have a recipe for Scotch Broth. We have tasted many but this has the simple and flavourful qualities we were looking for.

PREPARATION AND COOKING TIME: 3 hours 20 minutes
SERVES: 6

1.35 Kg (3lb) scrag end of mutton, or, if unavailable stewing lamb
3.6 litres (6 pints) water
Salt
2 tablespoons pearl barley, washed well
1 medium onion, finely chopped
1 leek, sliced
1 carrot, roughly chopped
1 turnip, peeled and roughly chopped
1 stick celery, roughly chopped
1 tablespoon finely chopped fresh flat-leaf parsley
freshly ground black pepper

Put the meat into a large saucepan with the water and 1 teaspoon of salt. Cover, bring to the boil and simmer gently for 2 hours. Add the barley and vegetables and simmer gently, covered, for another hour. Strain and return the broth to a clean saucepan. Cut the meat into small pieces, removing any fragments of bone, and return the meat and vegetables to the broth.
Reheat gently, stir in the parsley, taste for seasoning and serve.

CHAPTER SIX

Chilled

'Cold soups flooding the tongue with
soothing coolness, slowly contact
tastebuds which hot soups rarely reach,
permitting appreciation of
more delicate flavours'

Coralie Castle (from her book *Soup* 1971)

Summer Tomato Soup

This smooth creamy creation made with the ripest summer tomatoes was developed by Caroline Jeremy for the soup company's first ever Summer Range of lighter soups, designed to be perfect for chilled eating. Half size cartons of the soup bearing the name of each guest were served in large buckets of crushed ice at Caroline's wedding - where it was given the seal of approval.

If you like more unusual cookery ideas, why not try taking this soup one step further. We have given the recipe for Summer Tomato Sorbet, created by Mary Scott Morgan, the vegetarian caterer and broadcaster, who regularly regales her listener with lots of exciting ways to use our soups. It can be made with Summer Tomato in cartons or homemade.

PREPARATION AND COOKING TIME : 30 minutes
SERVES : 6

25g (1oz) butter
1 medium onion, finely chopped
1 garlic clove, finely chopped
a pinch of paprika
900g (2lb) ripe tomatoes,
            coarsely chopped
1 teaspoon lemon juice
350ml (12 floz) water
1 dessertspoon brown sugar,
        or to taste.

25ml (1floz) milk
1 tablespoon single cream
salt and freshly ground
black pepper

TO GARNISH:
150ml (¼ pint) natural yoghurt
3 tablespoons chopped fresh basil

Melt the butter and cook the onion and garlic gently until soft in a covered saucepan, without colouring. Add a pinch of paprika and the tomatoes and cook for 10 minutes over a moderate heat. Add the lemon juice, water and brown sugar to taste and simmer for 5 minutes. Cool a little, then purée in a liquidiser. Pass through a fine sieve into a clean saucepan. Stir in the milk and the cream and taste for seasoning. Chill well. Serve garnished with a swirl of yoghurt and sprinkled with chopped fresh basil leaves.

Summer Tomato Sorbet

PREPARATION TIME : 10 minutes plus freezing
SERVES: 4

570ml (1 pint) Summer Tomato Soup
60ml (4 tablespoons) vodka
10ml (2 teaspoons) sugar
salt and freshly ground black pepper to taste

TO GARNISH:
basil leaves

Mix together soup, vodka, sugar and seasoning. Either place in an ice-cream maker and churn until the mixture is a soft-scoop consistency; or place in freezer and beat at half-hourly intervals until the mixture is a soft-scoop consistency. Serve on a bed of basil leaves.

Ⓥ

Sorrel Soup

Our first kitchen trial of this soup was made from sorrel from our MD's garden. Although expensive to buy in the shops, sorrel grows like a weed and there was a plentiful supply for these small scale tests. When we needed large quantities to use in the factory, we had to have it specially grown by a market gardener and in the plants' first year the fresh, lemony soup was delicious. Unfortunately, we did not realise that sorrel is best when young and in the next year, when the plants began their second crop, we were forced to admit that the flavour was not as good. However, it is worth finding good sorrel because this soup, considered to be a classic in France (Potage Germiny), is very good. Its lemony flavour means the soup can also be used as a sauce with cold poached fish.

PREPARATION AND COOKING TIME: 15 minutes
SERVES: 6

> 40g (1½oz) butter
> 1 large onion, finely chopped
> 900ml (1½ pints) vegetable stock (see page 6)
> 225g (8oz) fresh sorrel leaves
> 225ml (8 floz) single cream
> Salt and freshly ground black pepper

TO GARNISH:
150ml (¼ pint) single cream
2 tablespoons fresh chervil leaves

Melt the butter and cook the onion gently until soft in a covered saucepan, without colouring. Add the stock and bring to the boil. Stir in the sorrel, cover and cook for about 1 minute until the leaves wilt. Cool a little, then purée in a liquidiser. Return to a clean pan, add the single cream and taste for seasoning. This soup is delicious hot or chilled, garnished with a swirl of cream and fresh chervil leaves.

Mustard and Cress Soup

I would be the first to admit that mustard and cress does not sound at all promising as a flavour for soup. I was a major sceptic but this soup is full of flavour with a light fluffy texture. The recipe is the result of years of work. Annual Recipe Development students came and went without success, but Nikki, this year's placement, finally cracked it. Unfortunately, we have not yet found a supplier who can sell us cut mustard and cress. Instead, we would have to employ a person to snip at it for twenty-four hours a day with nail scissors. We don't want to inflict such a terrible job on anybody, so sadly, you may never see this flavour in our cartons.

PREPARATION AND COOKING TIME : 30 Minutes
SERVES : 6

15g (½oz) butter
1 small onion, finely chopped
40g (1½oz) leek, thinly sliced
125g (4½oz) potato, peeled and chopped
700ml (1¼ pint) vegetable stock (see page 6)
200g (7oz) mustard and cress
½ teaspoon freshly grated nutmeg
salt and freshly ground black pepper
100ml (4 floz) milk
75ml (3 floz) single cream

TO GARNISH :
150ml (¼ pint) natural yoghurt
Mustard and cress

Melt the butter and cook the onion gently until soft, without colouring. Add the leek and potato and cook for a further 5 minutes. Add the stock and bring to the boil. Simmer for about 20 minutes until the vegetables are tender. Stir in the mustard and cress and nutmeg and taste for seasoning. Cool a little, then purée in a liquidiser with the milk and cream. Reheat gently and serve garnished with natural yoghurt and mustard and cress.

Ginger and Carrot Soup with Lime

Shirlee Posner, a long time friend of Alison Adcock who heads up our recipe development department, is a Senior Lecturer/Industrial Tutor in food studies at South Bank University. Through her, the soup company has built up strong links with the University and now annually gives one student the opportunity to work with Alison developing new recipes. During Shirlee's long career in food, previously as a chef then as a restaurant manager and consultant, she has amassed a vast recipe collection. This refreshing midsummer recipe was from a restaurant she visited in SOHO, New York in 1989.

PREPARATION AND COOKING TIME: 45 minutes
SERVES: 6

1 tablespoon sunflower oil
1 tablespoon, finely grated fresh ginger, about 20g (3/4 oz)
1 garlic clove, crushed
2 small onions, sliced
900g (2lb) carrots, sliced
900 ml (1½ pints) vegetable stock (see page 6)
juice of 1 lime
150ml (¼ pint) milk
150ml (¼ pint) double cream
salt and freshly ground black pepper

TO GARNISH:
very thin slices of lime
lime juice

Heat the oil and cook the ginger, garlic and onion gently for 10 minutes in a covered saucepan, without colouring. Add the carrots and the stock. Cover, bring to the boil and simmer for about 20 minutes, until the vegetables are tender. Cool a little, then purée in a liquidiser. Stir in the lime juice little by little to taste, then add the milk and cream and taste for seasoning. This soup is delicious served hot or chilled. Garnish with thin slices of lime and sprinkle lime juice on top.

Sweet Potato and Avocado Soup

This moussy soup contains no milk or cream but lots of other delicious ingredients that give it a refreshing light taste. At the Soup Company, we have tried to use sweet potatoes as we love their subtle flavour, which is included to such good effect in Caribbean stews— readily available in the Harrow Road near our offices. However, they always lose their wonderful sweetness when we cook them in our factory, leaving a rather boring mush. The sweet potatoes used in this soup are only lightly cooked so they appear at their best. For maximum flavour, use the orange-fleshed variety.

PREPARATION AND COOKING TIME: 25 minutes
SERVES : 6

350g (12oz) sweet potatoes, peeled and diced
1 small onion, finely chopped
1 litre (1¾ pints) water
2 medium ripe avocados, peeled and stoned
grated rind and juice of ½ lemon
grated rind and juice of 1 small orange
½ teaspoon ground mace
pinch salt

To GARNISH:
½ avocado, cut into fine dice
rind of 1 orange and 1 lemon

Simmer the potatoes and onion in plenty of salted water for about 15 minutes. Cool a little, then purée with the avocado flesh until smooth. Stir in the lemon and orange rind and juice, and the ground mace and salt. Serve well chilled, garnished with avocado dice and orange and lemon rind.

Iced Cucumber and Yoghurt Soup

Anybody who loves soup will have heard of Lindsey Bareham's encyclopaedic book 'A Celebration of Soup'. This recipe is simple but perfect for a blistering summer day- lighter than a gazpacho but full of flavour. Like the best recipes it has a convoluted history: the 'soup guru' got it from Simon Hopkinson, chef at Bibendum, who adapted it from an old cordon bleu recipe which may have originated from Lebanese cooking.

PREPARATION AND COOKING TIME: 50 minutes
SERVES: 6

1 teaspoon salt
1 large cucumber, about 350g (12oz),
  peeled, deseeded and cut into small dice
275ml (½ pint) plain yoghurt
275ml (½ pint) tomato juice
1 small garlic clove, finely chopped
570ml (1 pint) light chicken stock (see page 7)
leaves of 1 small bunch of fresh mint, finely chopped,
      reserving 6 small sprigs for the garnish
275ml (½ pint) single cream
Tabasco or chilli powder to taste
salt and freshly ground black pepper

TO GARNISH:
6 small sprigs of fresh mint

Sprinkle the salt onto the cucumber and leave to drain for 30 minutes. Wash the cucumber and squeeze out excess moisture in a clean tea towel.

Mix together the yoghurt, tomato juice, garlic, stock and mint and infuse for 30 minutes. Strain through a fine sieve.

Stir the cucumber into the yoghurt mixture along with the cream and Tabasco or chilli powder. Taste for seasoning. Chill very well and serve garnished with sprigs of mint.

From A Celebration of Soup, Lindsey Bareham, 1993

Ⓥ

Leek and Orange Soup

New Covent Garden Soup Company has highlighted the importance of seasonally appropriate food by producing distinct Summer and Winter Ranges. Gone are the days when going to a summer wedding meant having to stuff yourself full of food that was far too heavy and rich for a hot day. This is is the perfect starter for a summer wedding: very easy to make in advance, able to wait on the table while the guests queue up for the bridal line and most importantly, light and refreshing. If you're planning a wedding in a hurry and won't have time to cook, this soup looks set to make a regular appearance in cartons as one of our summer Soups of the Month.

PREPARATION AND COOKING TIME: 30 minutes
SERVES: 6

15g (½oz) butter
1 small onion, finely chopped
300g (11oz) leek, finely sliced
900ml (1½ pints) vegetable stock (see page 6)
1. teaspoon lemon juice
Juice of 2 large oranges
75ml (3floz) milk
50ml (2floz) single cream
salt and freshly ground black pepper

TO GARNISH:
150ml (¼ pint) crème fraîche
2 tablespoons chopped fresh chives

Melt the butter and cook the onion until soft, without colouring. Add the leek and cook for 5 minutes. Add the vegetable stock, lemon and orange juice. Simmer until the vegetables are tender. Cool a little. Purée the soup in a liquidiser with the milk and cream and taste for seasoning. Serve chilled, garnished with a swirl of crème fraîche and a sprinkling of chopped chives.

Avocado and Cucumber Soup

This summer green salad made into a soup is the invention of our Recipe Development placement student Nikki Martin from South Bank University. Her brief was to create an avocado soup for our summer range, and after combining avocado with almost every ingredient she could think of, she hit the jackpot with this one. Light, delicious and elegant - don't wait for our version in cartons - make it yourself!

PREPARATION AND COOKING TIME: 30 minutes
SERVES: 6

15g (½ oz) butter
1 small onion, finely chopped
3 large ripe avocados, peeled and stoned
1 teaspoon lemon juice
900ml (1½ pints) vegetable stock (see page 6)
150g (5oz) cucumber, chopped
75ml (3 floz) milk
50ml (2 floz) single cream
salt and freshly ground black pepper

TO GARNISH:
1 tablespoon each of cucumber, avocado and tomato, cut into fine dice

Melt the butter and cook the onion gently until soft, without colouring. Mash the avocado to a pulp, mix with the lemon juice and stir into the onion. Add the stock and cucumber. Simmer for 5 minutes. Cool a little, then purée with the milk and cream in a liquidiser. Taste for seasoning. Chill well. Serve garnished with the cucumber, avocado and tomato dice.

Green Pea Lettuce and Mint Soup

When Caroline our Marketing Director, was away having her first baby, most of the work on that year's Summer Range fell solely to Alison, our Recipe Development Manager. Casting her mind around for ideas, she remembered 'petit pois à la Francais', her favourite side dish of peas, baked in the oven with lettuce, sugar and garlic. It made a delicious soup that can be eaten hot or cold, which has appeared in Summer Range lists ever since. The version below has fresh mint added for extra flavour.

PREPARATION AND COOKING TIME: 45 minutes
SERVES: 6

50g (2oz) butter
2 small onions, finely chopped
1 garlic clove, crushed
350g (12oz) potatoes, peeled and roughly chopped
900ml (1½ pints) light chicken stock (see page 7)
2 handfuls lettuce leaves, about 200g (7oz)
125g (4½oz) shelled fresh green peas,
        or, if unavailable, frozen peas
leaves of 1 small bunch of mint, shredded
150ml (¼ pint) single cream
salt and freshly ground black pepper

TO GARNISH:
2 tablespoons finely chopped fresh flat-leaf parsley

Melt the butter and cook the onions and garlic gently until soft in a covered saucepan, without colouring. Add the potatoes and stock. Cover, bring to the boil and simmer gently for about 20 minutes until the vegetables are tender. Add the lettuce leaves, peas and mint. Cover and simmer for a further 5 minutes. Cool a little, then purée the soup in a liquidiser. Stir in the cream and add a little more water if necessary to achieve the desired consistency. Taste for seasoning and chill well. Serve sprinkled with chopped fresh parsley.

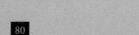

Gazpacho

Our decision to create a Gazpacho came just before Recipe Development Manager Alison Adcock's holiday in the Spanish region of Andalucia. Renowned for her dedication to the job, Alison valiantly tasted Gazpacho at every restaurant she visited and found that each area had its own subtly different version. On her return, she combined all the best qualities of the Spanish recipes and this is the result— for true authenticity, serve from a large bowl with a chunk of ice floating in the soup. Remember, proper Gazpacho has a strong flavour of garlic and red wine vinegar.

PREPARATION AND COOKING TIME: 1 hour
SERVES: 6

4 garlic cloves
50g (2oz) fresh white breadcrumbs
6 tablespoons red wine vinegar
6 tablespoons extra virgin olive oil
900g (2lb) sweet ripe tomatoes, peeled, deseeded and finely chopped
2 cucumbers, peeled, deseeded and finely chopped
225g (8oz) spring onions, thinly sliced
110g (4oz) red pepper, deseeded and finely chopped
110g (4oz) yellow pepper, deseeded and finely chopped
4 tablespoons chopped fresh herbs:
       parsley, basil or majoram
570ml (1 pint) iced water
½-1 teaspoon Tabasco, to taste
salt and freshly ground black pepper

TO GARNISH:
3 tablespoons croûtons (see page 108
   but do not toss in Parmesan cheese)

Using a pestle and mortar or a liquidiser, purée the garlic, breadcrumbs, vinegar and oil. Transfer to a bowl and stir in the tomatoes, cucumber, spring onions, red and yellow pepper and fresh herbs. Add the iced water and Tabasco and taste for seasoning. Purée one quarter of the soup in a liquidiser and return to the remaining soup. Chill well and serve offering croûtons to your guests.

(V)

Vichyssoise

When we serve this classic soup at shows and exhibitions, we always have to subtitle it 'Leek and Potato' because surprisingly, many people have never heard of it. Many believe it to be a fish soup as in 'Fishy Soise' which seems to put them off trying it! Our version mirrors our best selling carton version which is good either hot or chilled.

PREPARATION AND COOKING TIME: 40 minutes
SERVES: 6

50g (2oz) butter
450g (1lb) leeks, finely sliced
225g (8oz) potatoes, peeled and thinly sliced
570ml (1 pint) water
275ml (10floz) milk
75ml (3floz) single cream
Salt and ground white pepper

TO GARNISH:
150ml (¼ pint) natural yoghurt

Melt the butter and cook the leeks and potatoes gently for 10 minutes in a covered saucepan, without colouring. Add the water, cover, bring to the boil and simmer for about 20 minutes until the vegetables are tender. Cool a little, then purée in a liquidiser. Stir in the milk and cream and taste for seasoning. Chill very well.
Serve garnished with a swirl of yoghurt.

CHAPTER SEVEN

Warming

'The Italian composer, Giuseppe Verdi,
gracefully attributed much of his inspiration
to the warming and sustaining effects
of a large bowl of soup'

The International Wine and Food Society's Guide to Soups, Robin Howe, 1967

Cheese Soup with Crispy Bacon

This sounds like the sort of dish that will 'lie heavily' in the stomach - delicious to eat but to be regretted later. While it should be reserved for cold weather eating, it is not as rich as it sounds - a sort of light English fondue that is popular with all, especially children.

PREPARATION AND COOKING TIME: 40 minutes
SERVES: 6

15g (½oz) butter
1 large onion, finely chopped
1 garlic clove, crushed
700g (1½lb) potato, peeled and roughly chopped
900ml (1½ pints) vegetable stock (see page 6)
6 rashers bacon, diced
110g (4oz) mature Cheddar cheese, grated
50ml (2floz) single cream
salt and freshly ground black pepper

TO GARNISH:
reserved crisp bacon

Melt the butter and cook the onion gently until soft, without colouring. Add the garlic, potato and vegetable stock. Bring to the boil and simmer for about 20 minutes until the vegetables are tender. Meanwhile, fry the bacon dice until crispy.

Purée the soup in a liquidiser and pour into a clean pan. Add the Cheddar cheese and cream and reheat gently. Stir in the bacon, reserving a little for the garnish. Taste for seasoning. Serve sprinkled with a little bacon.

Twitcher's Tail

Annette Bond was a finalist in our 1995 'Create a Soup' Competition with this delicious version of oxtail soup. It was much loved by everyone at our Hythe Road offices who tasted it during the preliminary judging. Here she describes how this soup got its name: 'I have only just become interested in soupmaking; in fact "Twitcher's Tail" was my first homemade soup. The name came about as I have two young children, Louise and Russell, and if I had said 'oxtail soup' they would have asked where oxtail came from. I thought "Twitcher's Tail" would allow their imagination to roam, thus reducing the need to ask questions.'

PREPARATION AND COOKING TIME: 3 hours 15 minutes
SERVES: 6

3 tablespoons extra virgin olive oil
700g (1½lb) oxtail, cut into 4cm (1½in) pieces
1 medium onion, sliced
1 garlic clove, crushed
2 sticks celery, cut into 2.5cm (1in) lengths
1.2 litres (2 pints) beef stock (see page 9)
275ml (½ pint) red wine
1 tablespoon soy sauce
dash of Worcestershire sauce
2 bay leaves
40g (1½oz) finely chopped fresh flat-leaf parsley
2 tablespoons chopped fresh thyme
freshly ground black pepper

TO GARNISH:
150ml (¼ pint) soured cream
grated rind of 1 orange
2 tablespoons finely chopped fresh flat-leaf parsley

Pre-heat the oven to 150°C/300°F/Gas Mark 2.

Heat the oil and brown the segmented oxtail over a high heat. Remove from the pan. In the same pan, cook the vegetables gently for 5 minutes, covered, without colouring. Add the oxtail, and the remaining ingredients. Cover and bake in the oven for 2-3 hours. Allow to cool. Fork the meat off the oxtail, discard any fat, bone, sinew etc., and return to the soup. Reheat gently and serve garnished with a swirl of soured cream and a little grated orange rind and chopped fresh parsley.

Lamb and Irish Guinness Soup

This is a sort of Irish 'Scotch Broth' with the title ingredient responsible for its rich deep flavour. The recipe is especially appropriate for this book as the UK's Guinness brewery is just down the road from our Hythe Road factory at Park Royal. Apparently, the Irish believe that Guinness brewed in the Emerald Isle is far superior to anything that London can produce. Maybe they would approve of the latter being used as a cooking ingredient!

PREPARATION AND COOKING TIME: 2 hours
SERVES: 6

2 tablespoons extra virgin olive oil
2 medium onions, finely chopped
275g (10oz) boned shoulder of lamb, finely diced
1.2 litres (2 pints) beef stock (see page 9)
275 ml (½ pint) Guinness
3 sticks celery, diced
3 carrots, diced
50g (2oz) pearl barley, washed
110g (4oz) red lentils, washed
3 medium potatoes, about 450g(1lb), peeled and diced
pinch of dried mixed herbs
salt and freshly ground black pepper

TO GARNISH:
150ml (¼ pint) natural yoghurt
6 fresh basil leaves

Heat the oil and cook the onion over a moderate heat until golden. Remove the onion and, in the same pan, brown the lamb dice. Stir in the stock and Guinness. Return the onion to the pan and add the celery, carrots, barley and lentils. Partially cover and simmer for 1 hour, stirring from time to time. Add the potatoes and herbs, taste for seasoning and simmer for a further 10-15 minutes until the potatoes are tender. Serve garnished with a dash of yoghurt and basil leaves.

Smoked Haddock Chowder

The New Covent Garden Soup Company regularly have a tasting stand at county shows around the country to introduce people to our ever-changing flavours. At one of these, a man called Hugh Forestier Walker, owner of a poultry and game smoking company, told us about a delicious smoked stock that he was producing as a by-product of his smoking process. The recipe development team tasted it, loved it and developed this recipe to make good use of it. Although you can't buy this stock in small quantities for home-cooking, this chowder is still delicious made at home without the aforementioned ingredient – warming, substantial and full of flavour.

PREPARATION AND COOKING TIME: 40 minutes
SERVES: 6

25g (1oz) butter
1 small onion, finely chopped
400g (14oz) potatoes, peeled and roughly chopped
725ml (1¼ pints) fish stock (see page 8)
200g (7oz) natural uncooked smoked haddock,
skinned and flaked
75ml (3 floz) single cream
salt
cayenne pepper

TO GARNISH:
1 egg, hard-boiled and finely chopped
2 tablespoons finely chopped fresh flat leaf parsley

Melt the butter and cook three-quarters of the onion and 225g (8oz) of the potatoes gently for 5 minutes in a covered saucepan, without colouring. Add the stock, cover, bring to the boil and simmer gently for about 15 minutes until the vegetables are tender. Cool a little, then purée in a liquidiser. Return the soup to a clean pan, add the remaining vegetables, cover and simmer gently for about 10 minutes until the vegetables are tender. Add the fish, stir in the cream and add salt and cayenne to taste! Take care as the smoked haddock is quite salty already. Add more water if necessary to achieve the desired consistency. Serve garnished with chopped hard-boiled egg and chopped fresh parsley.

Roasted Tomato and Red Pepper Soup

We love roasted vegetables and here is yet another soup using them. Rachel Adcock, sister-in-law of Alison, (our Recipe Development Manager), and professional caterer, gave us this recipe which is easy and delicious. Incidentally, it is the same recipe that Caroline, the soup company's Marketing Director, gave out when she was interviewed on Debbie Thrower's Radio programme on Radio 2. Suddenly, without warning, Debbie turned to her and asked her for a soup recipe live on-air, Caroline successfully improvised the following:

PREPARATION AND COOKING TIME: 1 hour 30 minutes
SERVES: 6

6 medium red peppers, halved and deseeded
8 ripe tomatoes, skinned and halved
2 tablespoons extra virgin olive oil
1 teaspoon sugar
salt and freshly ground black pepper
1 tablespoon chopped fresh basil
1 medium onion, finely chopped
1 garlic clove, crushed
900ml (1½ pints) vegetable stock (see page 6)

TO GARNISH:
3 tablespoons chopped fresh basil

Pre-heat the oven to 190°C/375°F/Gas Mark 5

Place the red peppers skin side up in a roasting tin. Place the tomatoes cut side up in the same roasting tin, drizzle with 1 tablespoon of the olive oil and sprinkle with sugar, a pinch of salt and black pepper and the chopped fresh basil. Bake for 1 hour.

Heat the remaining olive oil and cook the onion and garlic very gently for 15 minutes in a covered saucepan, without colouring. Add the peppers and tomatoes. Add the stock, cover and bring to the boil. Cool a little then purée in a liquidiser. Taste for seasoning. Serve warm or chilled, garnished with lots of chopped fresh basil.

Hamisha Chicken Soup

Giselle Okin works as a planner at our advertising agency, Bartle Bogle Hegarty, famous for creating the Levi Jeans TV advertisements. Here is the soup's history: 'I can't cook to save my life. I can barely open a can of baked beans, but if I hadn't learnt to make chicken soup, my mother would never have forgiven me. This recipe is a family heirloom, I had to ask my mum's permission to offer it for public consumption (so to speak). As well as tasting good, a bowlful of chicken soup cures the common cold, mild depression and hair loss, amongst other things. To serve it in true "Jewish mother" style, you must remember to force a second bowl on guests whether they are still hungry or not!'

PREPARATION AND COOKING TIME: 2¼ hours
SERVES: 6

½ a plump chicken
1 medium turnip, peeled and halved
1 small parsnip, peeled and halved
2 garlic cloves, whole
1 bouquet garni
1.7 litres (3 pints) light chicken stock (see page 7)
1 medium swede, peeled and chopped
3 medium carrots, chopped
3 medium leeks, chopped
2 medium onions, chopped
4 sticks celery, chopped
Salt

MATZO BALLS:
fat from the soup
110g (4oz) matzo meal
salt and freshly ground black pepper
grated onion to taste (optional)
1 egg
2 tablespoons of the soup

Put the chicken into a large saucepan and add the turnip, parsnip, garlic cloves, bouquet garni and add light chicken stock to cover. Cover and bring to the boil. Skim off any scum. Simmer very gently for about 1 hour until there is a layer of fat on the surface. With a large spoon, transfer most of the fat to a bowl as this will be used to make the matzo balls. Add the remaining vegetables, cover and simmer for another hour until the vegetables are tender. Add salt to taste.

To make the matzo balls, mix all the ingredients and add a little more matzo meal if the mixture is too sticky. Naturally if the mixture is too dry, add a little more soup until the right consistency is achieved. Allow to stand for a few minutes. Roll the mixture into small balls with floured hands.

Remove the vegetables from the soup, squashing them and squeezing any juices back into the soup. Throw away the turnip, parsnip and garlic and put the rest of the vegetables back into the soup. Remove the chicken meat from the bones and return to the soup. Reheat and when the soup is very hot, add the matzo balls. Simmer for about 3-5 minutes until the egg noodles are cooked and the matzo balls turn whitish and bob to the surface. Serve.

Onion Panade

A panade is a French country dish of soup-soaked bread. Caroline Jeremy, one of the New Covent Garden Soup Company's founders and now Marketing Director, swears by this recipe that she learnt while cooking in Paris. Layers of caramelised onions, bread and cheese are cooked together into a soupy mush that everybody likes. Caroline's sons Oscar and Edward are big fans.

**PREPARATION AND COOKING TIME: 2 hours 30 minutes
SERVES : 6**

50g (2oz) butter
4 large Spanish onions, thinly sliced (about 700g/1½lb)
salt
250g (9oz) stale sourdough bread, thinly sliced
150g (5oz) freshly grated Parmesan and Gruyère cheese
lightly salted boiling water
2 tablespoons Cognac
shavings of butter

Pre-heat the oven to 180°C/350°F/Gas Mark 4

Melt the butter and cook the onions very gently, stirring occasionally, for about 1 hour, keeping them covered for first 40 minutes. After 1 hour, they should be caramelising lightly. Turn up the heat a little and cook for a further 10 minutes, stirring, to obtain a uniform rich caramel colour.

Spread the slices of bread thickly with the onions and then, using a large ovenproof dish, put a slice of bread onto the base. Sprinkle over a thick layer of cheese and repeat the process, packing each layer gently and avoiding empty spaces, until the dish is three-quarters full. Put a final layer of plain bread on top and sprinkle with cheese.

Slowly pour boiling water down the side of the dish, permitting the bread to swell and the mass to rise, until just floating. Bake in the pre-heated oven for 20 minutes. Take the dish out of the oven and add a little more boiling water. Sprinkle over a little more cheese, a little Cognac and shavings of butter, and bake for 30 minutes, until it is covered with a rich golden crust. Cool a little before serving.

Celery and Cashew Nut Soup

What do you get when you combine two opposites like healthy celery and super-calorific cashews? Answer! a delicious soup that is one of our favourites in this book. It has also been a firm favourite with Samantha Rowell's family ever since she invented it. She says: 'I would advise anyone who isn't a lover of celery or cashew nuts to give it a try. My husband doesn't like either but loves my soup'.

PREPARATION AND COOKING TIME: 45 minutes
SERVES: 6

75g (3oz) butter
2 heads of celery, roughly chopped
4 garlic cloves, finely chopped
150g (5oz) unsalted cashew nuts
1.5 litres (2½ pints) vegetable stock (see page 6)

TO GARNISH:
50g (2oz) unsalted cashew nuts, chopped
celery leaves

Melt the butter and cook the celery and garlic gently for 10 minutes in a covered saucepan, without colouring. Grind the nuts finely in a food processor and add to the pan along with the stock. Cover, bring to the boil and simmer for about 30 minutes until the vegetables are tender. Cool a little, then purée in a liquidiser. Pass the soup through a sieve into a clean saucepan.

For the garnish, put the cashew nuts into a frying pan over a high heat. Shake frequently until the nuts brown. Cool.

Reheat the soup gently and serve garnished with toasted chopped cashew nuts and chopped celery leaves.

Goulash Soup

Enthusiastic skiers will know that goulash eaten high in the Austrian mountains for lunch is one of the most delicious and warming meals that it is possible to eat. Developed by Alison, our Recipe Development Manager, lots of work went into making sure that this soup was as authentic as possible. Unfortunately, a peculiarly hot batch of chillis had been delivered to us just as we were going to launch the soup and an urgent discussion was needed. Consequently, Alison sent a motorcycle courier loaded with the first batch of Goulash soup to Caroline, our Marketing Director, at three 'o'clock in the morning!

PREPARATION AND COOKING TIME : 50 minutes
SERVES: 6

1 tablespoon beef dripping or sunflower oil
1 medium onion, finely chopped
1 garlic clove, crushed
350g (12oz) potatoes, peeled and diced
110g (4oz) tinned chopped tomatoes
75g (3oz) tomato purée
900ml (1½ pints) beef stock (see page 9)
150g (5oz) beef chuck steak, finely diced
150ml (¼ pint) red wine
50g (2oz) carrots, finely diced
50g (2oz) red pepper, finely diced
50g (2oz) green pepper, finely diced
2 heaped teaspoons paprika
1 teaspoon cayenne, or to taste
salt and freshly ground black pepper.

Heat the oil and cook the onion and garlic gently for 5 minutes in a covered saucepan, without colouring. Add the potatoes, tomatoes, tomato purée, stock, half the chuck steak, the red wine, carrots, red and green pepper, paprika, cayenne, salt and pepper, and simmer gently until the meat and vegetables are tender. Cool a little, then purée half the soup coarsely and half the soup smoothly in a liquidiser. If necessary add a little water to achieve the desired consistency. Return to a clean saucepan and add the remaining meat. Cook for 15 minutes, then taste for seasoning and serve.

Puy Lentil with Thyme Soup

Although these large blue-green lentils have long been around in French cuisine, they have only recently come to the fore in the UK, championed by fashionable restaurants and Delia Smith. This soup was originally 'Lamb with Puy Lentils' but because it was too expensive to use good quality lamb, we decided that the lentils should go it alone. The result has a rich earthy flavour very different from ordinary lentil soup. Try the stunning roast vegetable and anchovy garnish if you are entertaining, as it takes this soup to gourmet heights.

PREPARATION AND COOKING TIME: 50 minutes
SERVES: 6

25g (1oz) butter
1 medium onion, finely chopped
1 garlic clove, crushed
175g (6oz) carrots, chopped
90g (3½ oz) potatoes, peeled and chopped
110g (4oz) red lentils, washed
60g (2½ oz) Puy lentils, washed
900ml (1½ pints) vegetable stock (see page 6)
2 teaspoons chopped fresh thyme
salt and freshly ground black pepper

TO GARNISH:
25g (1oz) aubergine, cut into 4cm (1½ in) strips
25g (1oz) courgette, cut into 4cm (1½ in) strips
25g (1oz) red pepper, cut into 4cm (1½ in) strips
25g (1oz) yellow pepper, cut into 4cm (1½ in) strips
2 tablespoons extra virgin olive oil
4 anchovy fillets, finely chopped

Pre-heat the oven to 200°C/400°F/Gas Mark 6.

Melt half the butter and cook three-quarters of the onion and the garlic gently until soft in a covered saucepan, without colouring. Add the carrots, half the potatoes, the red lentils, vegetable stock and thyme. Cover, bring to the boil and simmer for 15 minutes until the vegetables are tender. Cool a little, then purée in a liquidiser.

Melt the remaining butter and cook the remaining onion and potatoes gently for 3 minutes, stirring occasionally to prevent the potatoes from sticking to the base of the pan. Add to the puréed soup along with the Puy lentils. Cover and simmer gently for 20 minutes. Taste for seasoning.

For the garnish, toss the vegetables in the oil, put in a roasting tin and roast in the oven for about 20 minutes until brown at the edges. Cool and mix gently with the anchovies.

Serve the soup garnished with the roasted vegetables and chopped anchovies.

Red Pepper and Goats' Cheese Soup

If you like the distinctive taste of goats' cheese, you should make this soup. The flavour of the cheese is not lost but enhanced by the sweet fresh pepper which also gives this soup its wonderful colour. Carina Mann entered this for our Good Housekeeping competition but has since moved house so if you happen to know her, please tell her that we have borrowed her recipe to use here.

PREPARATION AND COOKING TIME: 1 hour
SERVES: 6

2 medium onions, finely chopped
1.7 litres (3 pints) vegetable stock (see page 6)
75 ml (3 fl oz) dry white wine
8 medium red peppers, deseeded and coarsely chopped
1 large cooking apple, peeled, cored and coarsely chopped
2 teaspoons dried basil
salt and freshly ground black pepper
150g (5oz) soft rindless goats' cheese

TO GARNISH:
½ baguette, cut into 2cm (3/4 in) slices
110g (4oz) soft rindless goats' cheese

Boil the onions in 5floz (¼ pint) stock for about 10–15 minutes until the stock has evaporated and the onions have browned and are beginning to stick to the bottom of the pan, but do not burn them. Add the wine, scraping all the brown bits off the bottom of the pan, and simmer for 3 minutes. Add the red peppers, apple, basil, salt, pepper and the remaining stock and simmer, partially covered, for about 30 minutes until the vegetables are tender. Cool a little, then purée in a liquidiser. Pass the soup through a sieve into a clean saucepan and reheat gently. Add the goats' cheese and whisk into the soup until it has melted. Taste for seasoning.

For the garnish, toast the baguette slices and then spread each slice with the creamy goats' cheese. Finally grill the slices until the goats' cheese is bubbling and browning. Pop the croûtes on top of each bowl of soup and serve.

CHAPTER EIGHT

Exotic

Sexy Soup

Take one man and one woman (add more if so inclined)
Toss in a tangled mass of underwear for a couple of hours
Fill a large bath with warm water and carefully add a few drops
of lavender essence.
Take the couple (who should by now be well marinated in each
other's juices) and add them to the water.
Soak until they're both exhausted (or their extremities go wrinkly)
Serve.

Gary Martin, Bartle Bogle Hegarty 1995

Black-Eyed Bean Soup with Oregano

This soup came from a Nicola Cox recipe somebody tore out of Taste magazine, where it was called Black Bean Soup with Oregano. When Jo our recipe tester made it, she used black-eyed beans by mistake and the result was delicious, so we have amended the recipe for this book.

Well-known food writer, Nicola Cox, was inspired to create this recipe by a similar soup that she tried when lunching with her publisher at Jo Allen's, a restaurant in London's Covent Garden. Sometime afterwards she travelled to Venezuela to research new recipes and met a lady by the side of the road selling black beans—these were used to develop this recipe.

Make this recipe with either bean variety, try and get the chilli paste because it really makes a difference and don't forget the impressive chilli croûte garnish.

PREPARATION AND COOKING TIME: 2 hours 10 minutes
SERVES: 6

350 g (12oz) black-eyed beans, washed and
                 soaked in cold water overnight
1 medium onion, roughly chopped
1 medium carrot, roughly chopped
1 stick celery, roughly chopped
1.4 litres (2½ pints) light chicken or vegetable stock (see page 7 & 6)
1-2 garlic cloves, chopped
3 tablespoons tomato purée
3 teaspoons Mexican chilli paste
salt and freshly ground black pepper
2 teaspoons chopped fresh oregano

TO GARNISH:
1 tablespoon sunflower oil
2-3 rashers smoked streaky bacon, chopped
2 tablespoons finely chopped fresh oregano

Place the drained beans, onion, carrots and celery in a large pan with the stock, garlic, tomato purée and chilli paste. Cover and simmer gently for about 2 hours or until the beans are tender, adding the salt and oregano 10-15 minutes before the beans are completely cooked.

Meanwhile, heat the oil for the garnish and sauté the onions over a moderate heat until crisp. Drain on kitchen paper.

Purée half of the soup in a liquidiser and mix with the other half in the saucepan. Add water if necessary to achieve the desired consistency and taste for seasoning. Reheat and serve sprinkled with crisp bacon and chopped fresh oregano.

From Creative Food Processor Cookery, Nicola Cox, Ebury Press, 1986

Ttoro Basque

This is the Basque version of the classic soup-stew Bouillabaisse, using a slightly different combination of fish and seafood. The recipe was given to us by Iris Guilloux from Biarritz, who worked in our sales department recently - she got it from her mother.

PREPARATION AND COOKING TIME: 40 minutes
SERVES: 6

900g (2lb) mixed fish and shellfish, e.g. whiting, mackerel, bass, crab, prawns, mussels, langoustine, eel etc.
150ml (¼ pint) extra virgin olive oil
2-3 medium onions, finely sliced
2 sticks celery, chopped
225g (8oz) tomatoes, skinned and sliced
2 garlic cloves, crushed
1 bay leaf
1 sprig of fresh thyme
a few fresh parsley sprigs
rind of ½ orange, cut into very fine strips
salt and freshly ground black pepper
a pinch of saffron shreds dissolved in 1 tablespoon water
a pinch of cayenne pepper
salt and freshly ground black pepper

Wash the fish and pat dry with kitchen paper. Fillet and skin the fish if necessary and cut into large, thick pieces. Remove any shellfish from their shells.

Heat the oil and cook the onion and celery gently for 5 minutes in a covered saucepan, without colouring. Add the remaining ingredients together with the fish in a layer, then add just enough water to cover. Cover, bring to the boil and simmer very gently for 5 minutes. Add the shellfish and cook for a further 5 minutes. Taste for seasoning and serve.

Persian Yoghurt Soup

The source of this traditional recipe from the Middle East is an Iranian ex-patriot living in the UK, who would prefer to remain nameless. The soup is, therefore, completely authentic and must be very successful in reminding its author of her homeland.

PREPARATION AND COOKING TIME: 1 hour 10 minutes
SERVES: 6

1.2 litres (2 pints) water
225g (8oz) minced beef
1 large onion, sliced
75g (3oz) yellow split peas, soaked for 1 hour
                in plenty of water
½ teaspoon ground turmeric
½ teaspoon freshly ground black pepper
1 teaspoon salt
225g (8oz) long-grain rice
350g (12oz) fresh spinach, chopped
25g (1oz) chopped fresh dill
75g (3oz) chopped green spring onion tops
150ml (¼ pint) natural yoghurt

TO GARNISH:
2 tablespoons sunflower oil
½ medium onion, finely sliced
1 tablespoon chopped fresh mint

Bring the water to the boil and add the beef, onion, yellow split peas, spices and salt. Cover and simmer gently for 30 minutes. Add the rice and simmer for a further 20 minutes, stirring occasionally. Add the chopped spinach, dill and spring onion tops and simmer for a further 10 minutes. Stir in the yoghurt. Season well.

For the garnish, and the garnish is essential with this soup, sauté the onion over a moderate heat until golden brown, then add the mint and cook for a further 5 minutes until crisp. Drain on kitchen paper.

Reheat the soup, but do not boil, and serve with the crisp onion and mint sprinkled on top.

Sweet Potato and Orange Soup

Sarah Randell, one of the people who develop our new soups, has been to New Zealand several times to visit her Kiwi boyfriend's family. Apparently, everybody eats sweet potatoes all the time over there, so she felt inspired to create this soup. The sweet, tropical flavour of the potatoes (not really potatoes at all, but tropical root vegetables) contrasts wonderfully with the citrus orange to produce a soup which is great to eat in the depths of winter. Its colour and flavour will remind you of the heat of an antipodean summer.

PREPARATION AND COOKING TIME: 50 minutes
SERVES: 6

20g (3/4 oz) butter
1 large onion, finely chopped
500g (1lb 2oz) sweet potatoes, peeled, of which
    375g (13oz) roughly chopped
    125g (4½ oz) 1cm (½ in) dice
200g (7oz) potatoes, peeled and roughly chopped
2 tablespoons freshly squeezed orange juice
700ml (1¼ pints) vegetable stock (see page 6)
½ teaspoon ground coriander
150ml (¼ pint) milk
Salt and freshly ground black pepper

TO GARNISH:
1 tablespoon sunflower oil
3 rashers of unsmoked streaky bacon
150ml (¼ pint) crème fraîche

Melt the butter and cook the onion gently until soft in a covered saucepan, without colouring. Add 375g (13oz) roughly chopped sweet potatoes, the potatoes, orange juice, vegetable stock and ground coriander. Cover, bring to the boil and simmer for about 30 minutes until the vegetables are tender. Cool a little, then purée with the milk in a liquidiser. Taste for seasoning. Return to a clean pan and stir in the sweet potato dice. Cover, bring to the boil and simmer gently for about 15 minutes until the sweet potatoes are tender.

Meanwhile, heat the oil and sauté the bacon until crisp over a moderate heat. Drain on kitchen paper.

Serve the soup garnished with tablespoons of crème fraîche and topped with crisp bacon. The soup is also delicious served chilled.

Sherba

A stew-soup which is a speciality of North Africa was sent in by Mr. El-Hadery as an entry for our 1995 'Create a Soup' competition. This spicy blend of tomatoes, chickpeas, pasta, onions and lamb is very easy, totally authentic and extremely delicious.

PREPARATION AND COOKING TIME: 1 hour 35 minutes
SERVES: 6

2 tablespoons extra virgin olive oil
1 large onion, finely chopped
275g (10oz) boned shoulder of lamb, cut into fine dice
¼ teaspoon chilli powder
1 teaspoon ground turmeric
1 teaspoon ground cinnamon
150g (5oz) tomato purée
1.5 litres (2¾ pints) water
1 teaspoon salt
1 x 420g (15oz) tin chickpeas, rinsed
2-3 dessertspoons tiny star-shaped pasta
3 teaspoons dried mint
juice of 1 lemon

TO GARNISH:
150ml (¼ pint) natural yoghurt
2 tablespoons finely chopped fresh flat-leaf parsley

Heat the oil and cook the onions gently until soft in a covered saucepan, without colouring. Add the meat and brown well. Add the spices and tomato purée. Cook for 2 minutes, stirring. Gradually add the water over a period of 15 minutes in order to maintain a thick consistency. Add the salt, cover and simmer for 30-40 minutes. Add the chickpeas and simmer for 5 minutes, then stir in the pasta and simmer for 7 minutes. Add the mint and simmer for 1 minute. Stir in the lemon juice and serve garnished with a swirl of natural yoghurt and sprinkled with chopped fresh parsley.

Nora Carey's Ajiaco Bogotano

Nora Carey is currently the Marketing Director of the Ritz-Escoffier Ecole de Gastronomie in Paris, one of the world's most highly regarded cookery schools. Previously she has had an enviable career in food which started when she attended the Ecole de Cuisine La Varenne as a stagaire, later becoming Assistant Director. It was there that she met our Marketing Director, Caroline Jeremy and they have been friends ever since. After assisting several well-known cookery writers with their books, she wrote her own, Perfect Preserves, at the same time as working with Terence Conran to develop the Blue Print Café and a number of shops at Butler's Wharf. Perfect Preserves is the sort of cookery book that one can look at for hours – full of ideas and beautiful colour photographs. This recipe, given to Nora by a Colombian friend, comes from the book and is a tribute to her devotion to food.

PREPARATION AND COOKING TIME: 1½ hours
SERVES: 6

1.3–1.5 Kg (3–3½lb) chicken, cut into 6-8 serving pieces
1.7 litres (3 pints) chicken stock (see page 7)
1 large onion, peeled
1 small bay leaf
½ teaspoon ground cumin seeds
1 teaspoon dried thyme
2½ teaspoons salt
600g (1lb 5oz) potatoes, peeled, finely sliced
3 large corn on the cob, cut into 5cm (2in) round
150ml (¼ pint) double cream
¼ teaspoon freshly ground black pepper

TO GARNISH:

1 avocado, peeled, stoned and thinly sliced
150ml (¼ pint) soured cream
5 teaspoons capers, drained, rinsed in cold water
   and squeezed dry

Put the chicken pieces into a large saucepan with the stock. Slowly, bring to a simmer, then skim off any impurities. Add the onion, bay leaf, cumin, thyme and salt and simmer gently for 30 minutes until the chicken is tender. Transfer the chicken to a warm serving dish. Remove the meat from the bones and cut into small pieces. Strain the cooking liquor and return it to a clean saucepan. Boil the stock over high heat until it is reduced by one-third. Add the potatoes and cook for 15 minutes until the potatoes are tender. Mash half of the potatoes against the side of the saucepan to thicken the soup. Add the corn and chicken pieces and simmer uncovered for 5-10 minutes. Stir in the cream and season with pepper. Serve garnished with avocado slices, soured cream and capers.

Crab Creole

Prudence Lamy's entry to our 1995 Good Housekeeping competition initially caught my eye because of its beautifully illustrated cover. The recipe sounded interesting so we tested it and it turned out to look and taste delicious. Prudence is, unsurprisingly, a book illustrator by profession and has a Mauritian husband who took her to live on the island for a while. There she learnt to cook the native cuisine which is a wonderful mixture of Creole French, Chinese and Indian. Remember to decorate the finished soup with whole crab claws, for as Prudence says: 'It must look exotic, this is the treat, the magic of the island which inspires the recipe'.

PREPARATION AND COOKING TIME: 40 minutes
SERVES: 6

FOR THE STOCK:

fish head and tail
prawn shells
crab shell and smaller legs
onion skin

2 cloves
1 bay leaf
2 litres (3½ pints) water

2 tablespoons sunflower oil
1 medium onion, finely chopped, retain skin for stock (see below)
15g (½oz) finely grated fresh root ginger
225g (8oz) very ripe tomatoes, peeled
a pinch of saffron threads
1 sprig of fresh thyme
1 tablespoon tomato purée
500g (1lb 2oz) fresh huss, retain head and tail for stock (see below)
500g (1lb 2oz) whole uncooked prawns, peeled, retaining shells for stock (see below)
1 whole cooked fresh crab, retain shell for stock (see below) and claws for garnish
200ml (7floz) dry white wine
a good pinch of sugar
900ml (1½ pints) fish stock (see below)
1 tablespoon chopped fresh flat-leaf parsley
2 tablespoons chopped fresh coriander
salt and freshly ground black pepper

TO GARNISH:

2 crab claws from the crab, with shell, to give to your special
    guests, unless your fishmonger has 4 additional crab claws

To make the stock, put all the stock ingredients into a large saucepan. Cover, bring to the boil and simmer for about 30 minutes, skimming from time to time. Cool and strain well.

Heat the oil and cook the onion gently until soft in a covered saucepan, without colouring. Add the ginger, tomatoes, saffron, thyme and tomato purée. Place the huss and prawns on top and then add the wine and sugar. Simmer gently, covered, for 5 minutes. Add the crabmeat, cover and simmer for a further 5 minutes. Pour on the fish stock, cover, bring to the boil, then add the parsley and coriander and taste for seasoning.

Serve at once, very hot, garnished with the crab claws.

Duck Noodle Soup

Noodle bars are all the rage in London at the moment. Noodles are the 90's equivalent of pasta, healthy and full of flavour. The following is a recipe from Sophie Grigson's excellent book 'Meat Course' which is one of our favourites in the soup company's cook book library. Once you've made the stock, the rest is easy and the result is a delicious meal full of exotic flavours

PREPARATION TIME: 15 minutes
STOCK COOKING TIME: 2 hours
SERVES: 6

FOR THE STOCK:

1 duck carcase and, if available, giblets (not liver) and skin
1 onion, quartered
1 carrot, sliced
2 celery sticks, sliced

1 bay leaf
3 sprigs of parsley
2 sprigs of thyme
6 black peppercorns

2.25 litres (4 pints) well-flavoured duck stock (see below) skimmed of all fat
3 tablespoons soy sauce
2½ tablespoons rice wine or dry sherry
2 tablespoons rice vinegar or cider vinegar
3 tablespoons demerara sugar
1 star anise
3 cloves
10cm (4 inch) cinnamon stick
2.5cm (1 inch) piece fresh root ginger, cut into fine matchsticks
2 carrots, cut into fine matchsticks
1 red chilli, seeded and cut into thin rings, or to taste
8 spring onions, shredded
1½ layers Chinese egg thread noodles
Scraps of duck from the carcass
175g (6oz) bean curd, cubed
Salt and freshly ground black pepper

To make the stock, put all the stock ingredients in a pan and cover generously with water. Bring up to the boil, then simmer gently for 2-3 hours, occasionally skimming off any scum that rises to the top. Add more boiling water if the liquid level drops too low. Strain and cool. If you have time, chill overnight in the fridge and lift off the congealed fat from the surface the next day. If not, then skim off as much fat as you can.

Put the stock into a saucepan with the soy sauce, rice wine, vinegar, sugar, star anise, cloves, cinnamon, and ginger. Cover, bring gently to the boil, add the carrots and simmer for 2 minutes. Add the chilli, spring onions and noodles. Simmer for 2 minutes until the noodles are cooked, then gently stir in the scraps of duck and the bean curd. Heat through for 1 minute, taste for seasoning and then serve.

From Sophie Grigson's Meat Course, 1995

Spicy Vegetable Soup with Peanut

We receive soup ideas from all over the world, so we were not surprised when a soup fan in Lesotho sent us a recipe for peanut soup. This was tested and felt to be too rich for British tastes although we liked the general principle of a nut-enriched soup. Fortunately, our placement student at that time, Shirley, was from Trinidad and had the idea of adding some vegetables and spice to the peanuts so the result was very similar to a soup that her mother often made. Now the recipe makes a regular appearance in our cartons and has become a cult flavour with a small but loyal band of our customers who buy it in bulk wherever they find it.

PREPARATION AND COOKING TIME : 40 minutes
SERVES: 6

2 medium onions, finely chopped
110g (4oz) crunchy peanut butter
350g (12oz) tinned chopped tomatoes
900ml (1½ pints) vegetable stock (see page 6)
175g (6oz) potatoes, peeled and chopped
75g (3oz) pimentos, drained weight
175g (6oz) carrots, chopped
75ml (3floz) single cream
cayenne to taste
paprika to taste

TO GARNISH:
2 tablespoons fresh coriander leaves

Gently cook the onions with the peanut butter and 1 tablespoon of water for 5 minutes in a covered saucepan, without colouring. Add the tinned tomatoes, vegetable stock, potatoes, pimentos and carrots. Cover, bring to the boil and simmer gently until the vegetables are tender. Stir in the cream and cayenne and paprika to taste. Serve sprinkled with fresh coriander leaves.

Moroccan Chickpea and Spinach Soup

As a winner of our 1996 Good Housekeeping competition, John Stephens was awarded a very smart designer stove and a week's course at the famous Ritz-Escoffier Ecole de Gastronomie Francais in Paris. These were the perfect prizes for an ex-accountant who left London to start up his own catering company, the Mill Kitchen in Otley. His soup is a fragrant, spicy taste of North Africa which was unanimously voted the winner by all the judges.

PREPARATION AND COOKING TIME: 1 hour
SERVES: 6

2 tablespoons extra virgin olive oil
3 medium onions, finely chopped
2 garlic cloves, crushed
1½ teaspoons ground cinnamon
1 teaspoon chilli powder, or to taste
2 tablespoons tomato purée
150g (5oz) dried apricots, chopped
finely grated rind of ½ lemon
4 teaspoons lemon juice
1.5 litres (2½ pints) vegetable stock (see page 6)
250g (9oz) chickpeas
200g (7oz) fresh spinach, shredded
salt and freshly ground black pepper

TO GARNISH:
150 ml (¼ pint) natural yoghurt

Heat the oil and cook the onions gently for 5 minutes in a covered saucepan, without colouring. Add the garlic and spices and cook, stirring, for 1 minute. Add the tomato purée and cook for 3 minutes. Add the apricots, lemon rind and juice, stock and chickpeas. Cover and simmer for about 20 minutes, until the chickpeas are tender. Cool a little then purée in a liquidiser. Return to a clean saucepan. Stir in the spinach, cover pan and simmer for a further 5 minutes until the spinach has wilted. Season to taste and serve garnished with a swirl of yoghurt.

Roast Red Pepper, Corn and Chilli Chowder

In 1995 the New Covent Garden Soup Company set up a company in the US to see how our soups would go down with the people of the San Francisco Bay Area. A limited range of soups was regularly flown out and a number of high-quality delicatessens were persuaded to stock them. At the beginning, the company consisted of only two employees, Alastair Dorward and Kathy West who had to do everything: sales, marketing, deliveries etc. This 'test market' was a great success, there are more people on board and the soup is now also available on the Eastern Seaboard. Kathy left and was replaced by Kelly Schaeffer, Marketing Manager, who sent us her family's chowder recipe.

PREPARATION AND COOKING TIME: 1 hour
SERVES: 6

3 medium fresh red chillies
2 medium red peppers
3 fresh ears of corn
1.2 litres (2 pints) light chicken stock (see page 7)
50g (2oz) butter
1 large onion, finely chopped
1 medium leek, white part only, sliced
1 garlic clove, crushed
2 medium potatoes, about 350g (12oz),
    peeled and roughly chopped
150 ml (¼ pint) single cream
Salt and freshly ground black pepper

TO GARNISH:
2 tablespoons chopped fresh chives
3 tablespoons croûtons (see page 108 but do not toss in Parmesan cheese)

Pre-heat the oven to 200°C/400°F/Gas Mark 6.

Put the chillies and red peppers into a roasting tin and bake in the oven for 30 minutes. Put the ears of corn into a saucepan with the stock. Cover, bring to the boil and simmer for 30 minutes.

Meanwhile, melt the butter and cook the onion, leek and garlic gently in a covered saucepan for 10 minutes, without colouring.

After 30 minutes, remove the chillies and red peppers from the oven and, when cool enough to handle, skin and deseed them, cutting the chillies into small dice and the red peppers into small even pieces and keeping them separate. Remove the ears of corn from the stock, remove the corn and reserve both stock and corn.

Add the chillies, potatoes and stock to the onion, leek and garlic mixture, cover, bring to the boil and simmer gently for about 15-20 minutes until the vegetables are tender. Add the cream, corn and red pepper pieces. Purée half the soup in a liquidiser and return to the soup in the saucepan. Taste for seasoning. Reheat gently and serve. Garnish with the chives and croûtons.

CHAPTER NINE

Seasonal

'New Covent Garden Soup Company believes in
using ingredients at their seasonal peak.
It was this belief that led them to produce
their ever-changing Soup of the Month recipes'

From a New Covent Garden Soup Company press release 1991

Jerusalem Artichoke and Spinach Soup

At the Soup Company we make an artichoke soup and a spinach soup of which we are proud. As a result, when Jo Gilks, our recipe tester, suggested this combination of the two that she had been making for years, I was a bit dubious. However, the beautiful emerald green colour and the light texture convinced me otherwise — a glamorous soup if ever there was one.

PREPARATION AND COOKING TIME: 40 minutes
SERVES: 6

175g (6oz) young spinach leaves
25g (1oz) butter
1 small onion, finely chopped
350g (12oz) Jerusalem artichokes, finely sliced
570ml (1 pint) light chicken stock (see page 7)
salt and freshly ground black pepper
freshly grated nutmeg
275ml (½ pint) milk
2 tablespoons double cream (optional)

TO GARNISH:
PARMESAN CROÛTONS
3 slices fresh white bread, crusts removed
1cm (½ in) sunflower oil
3 tablespoons freshly grated Parmesan cheese

Wash the spinach and remove the stalks. Melt the butter in a large saucepan and cook the onion gently until soft, covered, without colouring. Add the artichokes and continue to cook for 10 minutes, stirring from time to time to prevent the artichokes from sticking to the base of the pan. Add the stock and season with salt, pepper and nutmeg. Cover, bring to the boil and simmer gently for about 20 minutes until the artichokes are tender.

Meanwhile, make the Parmesan croûtons. Cut the bread into 1cm (½ in) dice. Heat the oil in a frying pan and, when very hot, fry the bread dice until crisp and golden. Put the Parmesan cheese on to a sheet of greaseproof paper and quickly toss the croûtons with the Parmesan, ensuring they remain separate and not too clogged with cheese.

Stir the spinach leaves into the soup and purée the soup in a liquidiser. Add the milk and cream, if using, and taste for seasoning. Reheat and serve with the Parmesan croûtons. The soup is also delicious served chilled

(v)

Grandad Elf's Spring Herb Soup

Julie Anne Towersey, a project co-ordinator for an international charity finds creating new recipes 'good for the body and soul after a hectic day at work' so she entered our 1995 'Create a Soup' competition. Her inspiration for this flavourful herb soup came from her great-grandparents, Grandad Elf and Nanny 2. Grandad Elf was a keen gardener who grew his own fruit and vegetables, and had a particular passion for herbs. Nanny 2 always had to come up with new and innovative ways to use his produce. Consequently this soup was created as a tribute to them both. Julie Anne says that whenever she makes it, it takes her back to when she was a little girl sitting by her great-grandparents' range waiting to see what was for tea.

PREPARATION AND COOKING TIME: 45 minutes
SERVES: 6

    25g (1oz) butter
    1 large onion, finely chopped
    1 garlic clove, crushed
    1 stick celery, finely chopped
    110g (4oz) red or brown lentils washed
    1.2 litres (2 pints) vegetable stock (see page 6)
    225g (8oz) fresh spinach
    1 tablespoon each
      chopped fresh flat-leaf parsley, chives,
      tarragon, thyme and majoram
    1 teaspoon lemon juice
    150ml (¼ pint) Greek yoghurt
    salt and freshly ground black pepper

TO GARNISH:
reserved Greek yoghurt
reserved chopped fresh herbs

Melt the butter and cook the onion, garlic and celery gently for a few minutes in a covered saucepan, without colouring. Add the lentils and stir to coat well. Add the stock, cover, bring to the boil and simmer for about 20-30 minutes until the lentils are soft. Reserving 1 tablespoon of the chopped herbs for the garnish, add the spinach and remaining herbs to the soup and cook for 1 minute until the spinach has wilted. Cool a little, then purée the soup in a liquidiser along with the lemon juice and most of the yoghurt, reserving 6 teaspoons of yoghurt and chopped herbs for the garnish.

Avocado Gazpacho

As a teacher of children with emotional and behavioural problems and with four children of her own, Jennifer Boarder occasionally hankers after a more hedonistic lifestyle of which this recipe would be part - simple, fresh and delicious. The inspiration comes from a spell living in California with its wonderful climate and quality fresh foods.

PREPARATION AND COOKING TIME: 25 minutes
SERVES: 6

570ml (1 pint) soured cream
275ml (½ pint) milk
570ml (1 pint) each of tomato juice and passata
4 tablespoons lemon juice
2 tablespoons extra virgin olive oil
2 garlic cloves, very finely chopped
2 bay leaves
2 cucumbers, peeled, deseeded and finely chopped
2 tomatoes, skinned, deseeded and cut into fine dice
Tabasco to taste
Salt
3 avocados, peeled and stoned
2 tablespoons lemon juice

TO GARNISH:
1 tablespoon sunflower oil
3 rashers thin unsmoked streaky bacon, finely sliced

Combine the soured cream, milk, tomato juice, passata, lemon juice, oil and garlic. Add the bay leaves, cucumber and tomatoes. Add the Tabasco and taste for seasoning. Chill well.

For the garnish, heat the oil and sauté the bacon over a moderate heat until crisp. Drain on kitchen paper.

Just before serving the soup, remove the bay leaves, mash the avocados with lemon juice and stir into the tomato mixture. Taste for seasoning and serve in chilled bowls sprinkled with crisp bacon.

Nick's Game and Chestnut Soup

Our Financial Director is the typical shooting and fishing type but is not known for his cooking. He claims to have a supply of women who are only too willing to cook for him when he goes down to his cottage at the weekends. Which one of them invented this recipe? I am sure we will never find out but thanks to her we have a delicious soup that even those who are not mad on game will enjoy.

PREPARATION AND COOKING TIME: 1 hour
SERVES: 6

450g (1lb) fresh chestnuts, peeled, or
        tinned chestnuts will do
1 tablespoon bacon fat or oil
1 medium carrot, roughly diced
1 onion, thinly sliced
1 stick celery, sliced
1 medium-sized potato, about 200g (7oz),
  peeled and roughly diced
scraps of cooked game meat
1.5 litres (2½ pints) game stock (see page 10)
1 bay leaf
1 sprig of fresh thyme
salt and freshly ground black pepper

TO GARNISH:
hot croûtons of fried bread
(see page 108 but do not toss in Parmesan cheese)

This is an ideal way of using up the carcass and scraps from roasted pheasant, partridge or grouse.

To peel chestnuts, either make a slit in the skins, place on a baking sheet and roast at 200°C/400°F/Gas Mark 6 for 20 minutes, then peel; or drop into boiling water, simmer for 15 minutes, drain and then peel.

Heat the fat or oil and cook the carrots, onion, celery and potatoes gently in a covered saucepan for 5 minutes, without colouring. Add the chestnuts and any cooked game. Cover with the stock and add the bay leaf and sprig of fresh thyme. Cover and simmer gently for about 40 minutes until the chestnuts and vegetables are very tender. Taste for seasoning and serve with hot croûtons.

Mussel, Red Pepper and Tomato Soup

Another recipe torn out of the paper, this substantial gourmet soup turned out to have been created by the famous cook Josceline Dimbleby for the Sunday Telegraph. Josceline tells me that she loves soups that, with good bread, can be eaten as a meal. This soup-meal was created one lunchtime at her holiday cottage in Devon where she can buy delicious, huge, yellow mussels fresh from the River Dart.

PREPARATION AND COOKING TIME: 1 hour 15 minutes
SERVES: 6

1.35 Kg (3lb) mussels
150ml (¼ pint) red wine
700g (1½lb) ripe tomatoes, skinned
1 small red pepper, halved and deseeded
75g (3oz) butter
2 large garlic cloves, finely chopped
1 heaped teaspoon paprika
40g (1½oz) plain flour
450ml (¾ pint) fish stock (see page 8)
150ml (¼ pint) double cream
Salt and freshly ground black pepper

Scrape any barnacles off the mussels with a knife and wash them very thoroughly. Put them into a large saucepan with the red wine, cover the pan and put over a high heat. Shake the pan for about 3 minutes or until most of the mussels have opened. Remove from the heat. Discard any mussels that have not opened. Strain well, reserving the cooking liquor.

Purée the skinned tomatoes and the deseeded red pepper in a liquidiser. Melt the butter over a moderate heat and stir in the garlic and paprika. Remove from the heat and stir in the flour. Gradually stir in the fish stock, the puréed tomatoes and red pepper and the strained mussel liquor. Put over a high heat and bring to the boil, stirring until the soup thickens. Cover the saucepan and simmer very gently for 30 minutes. Stir in the cream.

Reserve 18 open mussel shells with mussels attached. Remove the mussels from the remaining mussel shells. Add all the mussels to the soup. Serve the soup ensuring that each guest has 3 shells in their serving.

(V)

Kohlrabi with Caraway Soup

This recipe was the winner of the 1995 Good Housekeeping 'Create a Soup' Competition, in which Nicola Selhuber, a computer analyst from Northumberland, won the much coveted first prize of an Aga. Nicola grows her own vegetables and, by virtue of her Scots roots, is a keen soup maker.

We wanted to make the soup to launch with our 1995 Winter Range but there was a problem: we needed more than the UK's entire annual crop of kohlrabi to make enough cartons. Kohlrabi, a cross between a turnip and a cabbage which looks rather like a space alien, is much eaten on the continent but is not widely known here. Consequently, we asked one of our suppliers, Bedfordshire Growers, to grow the vegetable for us. Disaster struck, however, when the dry summer halted growth and near the end of the growing season the poor kohlrabi were still the size of golf balls. Thankfully, it eventually rained and the soup was launched at the end of September, proving popular until the crop was killed off by the first frost.

PREPARATION AND COOKING TIME: 40 minutes
SERVES: 6

> 25g (1oz) butter
> 450g (1lb) kohlrabi, peeled and chopped
> 40g (1½oz) plain flour
> 570 ml (1 pint) vegetable stock (see page 6)
> ½ medium onion, finely chopped
> 15g (½oz) finely chopped fresh flat-leaf parsley
> 2 level teaspoons caraway seeds
> 50ml (2floz) single cream
> salt and freshly ground black pepper

TO GARNISH:
1 tablespoon sunflower oil
3 rashers unsmoked streaky bacon

Melt the butter and cook the kohlrabi gently for 5 minutes in a covered saucepan, without colouring. Add the flour and stir for 1 minute. Still stirring, gradually add the stock. Cover, bring to the boil and simmer gently for about 20 minutes until the kohlrabi is tender. Cool a little, then purée in a liquidiser.

Boil the onion in plenty of water for 5 minutes, drain and add to the soup along with the parsley and caraway seeds. Cool, then stir in the single cream and taste for seasoning.

For the garnish, heat the oil and sauté the bacon over a moderate heat until crisp. Drain on kitchen paper.

Gently reheat the soup and serve garnished with crisp bacon.

PumpKin Soup

One of our favourite Soup of the Months, this soup always makes an appearance around Hallowe'en and goes well at themed parties. The homemade version is the perfect way to use what you have scooped out of your pumpkin lanterns. If you are entertaining, try serving the soup in the pumpkin shell as we have suggested – the larger, orange, American-style pumpkins taste better and have a larger shell.

PREPARATION AND COOKING TIME: 45 minutes
SERVES: 6

25g (1oz) butter
1 medium onion, finely chopped
200g (7oz) potatoes, peeled and chopped
900g (2lb) pumpkin, diced
250g (9oz) carrots, diced
1.2 litres (2 pints) vegetable stock (see page 6)
150ml (¼ pint) milk
demerara sugar to taste
finely grated nutmeg to taste
salt and freshly ground black pepper.

Melt the butter and cook the onion gently for 5 minutes in a covered saucepan, without colouring. Add the potato, 700g (1½lb) of the pumpkin, the carrots and the vegetable stock. Cover, bring to the boil and simmer gently for about 20 minutes until the vegetables are tender. Cool a little, then purée in a liquidiser. Return to a clean saucepan and stir in the milk.

Meanwhile, add the remaining pumpkin to a saucepan of boiling salted water and cook for 2 minutes. Drain and add to the puréed soup. Add the sugar, nutmeg and seasoning to taste. Reheat gently.

The most effective way to serve the pumpkin is in a hollowed-out pumpkin. Take a pumpkin and slice off the top quarter. Scoop out the seeds. Place slices of toasted baguette in the base together with grated Gruyère cheese. Fill with the soup, put on the lid and serve at the table.

Roasted Parsnip and Parmesan Soup

New Covent Garden Soup lover Marcus Batty, a managing director from Lincolnshire, has made a name for himself amongst family and friends for his roasted vegetables including mustard roast potatoes and Parmesan and garlic parsnips. When he saw our competition in Good Housekeeping magazine, he simply converted the latter recipe into a soup. The result is so delicious that it tastes like a classic that has been around for years. Maybe the real reason behind Mr Batty's endeavours is a need to prove his culinary skills to his bride-to-be: a very creative home economist!

PREPARATION AND COOKING TIME: 1 hour 10 minutes
SERVES: 6

450g (1lb) parsnips, cut into lengths
50g (2oz) freshly grated Parmesan cheese
2 tablespoons extra virgin olive oil
15g (½oz) butter
1 medium onion, finely chopped
1 tablespoon plain flour
1.35 litres (2¼ pints) light chicken stock (see page 7)
salt and freshly ground black pepper
4 tablespoons double cream

TO GARNISH:
freshly ground black pepper

Pre-heat the oven to 200°C /400°F/ Gas Mark 6

Simmer the parsnips in plenty of salted water for 3 minutes. Drain well and toss in half the Parmesan cheese. Put the olive oil in a roasting tin and heat in the oven for 3-4 minutes. Arrange the parsnips in the roasting tin, add the butter and bake for 45 minutes basting frequently. Drain the excess oil into a large saucepan and cook the onion gently until soft, without colouring. Stir in the flour and cook for 1 minute. Add the stock, stirring constantly, and bring to the boil. Add the parsnips. Simmer, covered, for 10 minutes.

Purée the soup with the remaining Parmesan cheese in a liquidiser. Stir in the cream, taste for seasoning and reheat. Serve garnished with twists of freshly ground black pepper.

Salsify with Mustard Seed Soup

A runner-up in our 1996 Good Housekeeping competition, Kerry Camm is a talented cook who had already won several other competitions before coming up with an excellent way to cook this unusual vegetable which looks like a thin light-brown carrot. Popular in Europe, the salsify's creamy white inner flesh combines very well with the almost crunchy mustard seed and the soup can be served either as a broth, or liquidised to a more creamy consistency.

PREPARATION AND COOKING TIME: 1 hour 15 minutes
SERVES: 6

50g (2oz) butter
1 large onion, finely chopped
1 tablespoon black mustard seeds
1 tablespoon white mustard seeds
1 Kg (2.2lb) salsify, scraped and chopped
1.5 litres (2½ pints) vegetable stock (see page 6)
salt and freshly ground black pepper
juice of 1 lemon

TO GARNISH:
150 ml (¼ pint) crème fraîche

Melt the butter and cook the onion gently for 5 minutes in a covered saucepan, without colouring. Add the mustard seeds and cook for 1 minute until they begin to pop. Add the salsify and cook for 3 minutes, stirring from time to time. Add the vegetable stock, cover, bring to the boil and simmer for about 20 minutes until the vegetables are tender. Taste for seasoning and add lemon juice to taste. Cool a little, then purée the soup roughly in a liquidiser. Reheat gently and serve with a swirl of crème fraîche.

Turkey and Cranberry Soup

Encouraged by her husband and mother-in-law, Deirdre Dookhie, an Abbey National Product Manager, entered this recipe with its own special stock for our 1995 'Create a Soup' competition. Made on Boxing Day from the inevitable Christmas leftovers, she says the flavour is subtly different every year. However, we think it makes a perfect winter soup, so why not try it across the season using some of the very good value turkey that is always in the shops.

PREPARATION AND COOKING TIME: 1 hour 30 minutes
SERVES: 6

FOR THE STOCK:
1 turkey leg on the bone, about 700g (1½lb)
6 cloves
6 peppercorns
2 bay leaves
1 mace blade
1 teaspoon salt
1 medium onion, halved
1 medium carrot, cut into large slices
1.5 litres (2½ pints) water

4 tablespoons olive oil
225g (8oz) each of parsnips, carrots and potatoes,
            cut into even-sized pieces
125g (4½oz) shallots, finely chopped
110g (4oz) fresh cranberries or 150g (5oz) dried cranberries
grated rind and juice of 1 orange
1 sprig fresh rosemary
1 sprig fresh thyme
125g (4½oz) Brussel sprouts, trimmed and roughly chopped
2 tablespoons finely chopped fresh flat-leaf parsley

TO GARNISH:
2 tablespoons finely chopped fresh flat-leaf parsley

To make the stock, place all the stock ingredients in a large saucepan. Cover, bring to the boil and simmer for about 1 hour until the meat is falling off the bone.

Meanwhile, heat the oil and sauté the parsnips, shallots, carrots and potatoes, stirring frequently, until evenly brown. Separately, cook the cranberries with the orange rind and juice until they burst. If using dried cranberries, soak them in the orange rind and juice for at least 30 minutes.

Strain the stock liquor and add this and the rosemary and thyme to the root vegetables. Then add the sprouts and half the cranberries. Cook for a further 5 minutes. Cool a little, then, having removed the sprigs of herbs, purée to the desired consistency.

Take the turkey meat off the bone and shred. Add to the soup with the remaining cranberries and parsley and taste for seasoning. Reheat gently before serving and garnish with chopped fresh parsley.

Brussels Sprout and Chestnut Soup

A well-known image of our company is the photo of William, our MD, in a pile of Brussels sprouts which appeared in our magazine advertising. The advert tells the story of how we created what became our Christmas Soup of the Month. William's farming family grow sprouts and he had the idea of making them into a soup. However, sprout soup alone would have a rather strong 'boiled cabbage' flavour so after a lot of experimentation, it was decided to team them with chestnuts. The result has been extremely popular but very seasonal, so if you are one of those who can not survive the rest of the year without a fix, here is the recipe.

PREPARATION AND COOKING TIME: 45 minutes
SERVES: 6

25g (1oz) butter
1 medium onion, finely chopped
250g (9oz) potatoes, peeled and chopped
1 Kg (2.2lb) Brussels sprouts, quartered
900ml (1½ pints) vegetable stock (see page 6)
50-110g (2-4 oz) fresh chestnuts to taste, skinned and crumbled or, if unavailable, tinned whole chestnuts
freshly grated nutmeg
150ml (¼ pint) milk
75ml (3 fl oz) single cream
salt and freshly ground black pepper

Peel the chestnuts: either make a slit in the skins, place on a baking sheet and roast at 200°C/400°F/ Gas mark 6 for 20 minutes, then peel; or drop into boiling water, simmer for 15 minutes, drain and then peel.

Melt the butter and cook the onion gently for 5 minutes in a covered saucepan, without colouring. Add the potatoes, 700g (1½lb) of the Brussels sprouts and the stock. Cover, bring to the boil and simmer gently for about 10 minutes until the vegetables are tender. Cool a little, then purée in a liquidiser.

Return to a clean saucepan and stir in the remaining Brussels sprouts, the chestnuts and nutmeg to taste. Cover, bring to the boil and simmer gently for about 5-10 minutes until the sprouts and chestnuts are tender. Stir in the milk and the cream, and add more water if necessary to achieve the desired consistency. Taste for seasoning, reheat and serve.

118

CHAPTER TEN

Sweet

'Of soup and love,
the first is best'

Thomas Fuller 1808-61

Ⓥ

Raspberry and Cranberry Soup

This fruit soup is easy to make, but looks very impressive with its swirl of sour cream. Sweet soups are the 'next big thing' in food fashion so if you want to try them but feel a bit nervous, this is the one for you.

PREPARATION AND COOKING TIME: 15 minutes
SERVES: 6

450g (1lb) fresh or frozen raspberries
725ml (1¼ pints) cranberry juice
3 teaspoons arrowroot
1 teaspoon lemon juice
25-50g (1-2oz) sugar

TO GARNISH:
150ml (¼ pint) soured cream

Liquidise two-thirds of the raspberries with the cranberry juice, reserving one tablespoon of cranberry juice. Pass through a sieve to remove the pips. Bring to the boil in a saucepan. In a separate bowl, mix the arrowroot and the tablespoon of cranberry juice until smooth. Pour the hot raspberry mixture over the arrowroot cream, stirring, and return the mixture to the saucepan. Stir over a gentle heat until the soup has thickened. Remove from the heat and add the remaining raspberries, a little lemon juice and sugar to taste. Chill.

Stir the soured cream to make it smooth and then serve each bowl of chilled soup with a swirl of soured cream.

Chocolate Soup

Reminiscent of 'Charlie and the Chocolate Factory', this only sounds bizarre because the word soup is usually associated with savoury flavours. In fact, the best way to think of this soup is like a more liquid chocolate mousse — serve in a coffee or tea cup on a saucer with a teaspoon and it looks very amusing and original. This recipe comes from one of our recent visits to new restaurants. The renowned chef, Eric Chavot, who has worked with Pierre Koffman, Raymond Blanc, Marco Pierre White and Nico Ladenis, recently opened the Interlude de Chavot in Charlotte Street in London to much acclaim, gaining a Michelin star within eleven months of opening — we loved this soup so much that we asked him for the recipe.

PREPARATION AND COOKING TIME: 30 minutes
SERVES: 6

725 ml (1¼ pints) milk
250 ml (9 floz) double cream
500g (1lb 2oz) good dark chocolate, coarsely chopped
50g (2oz) caster sugar
8 egg yolks
200ml (7 floz) whipping cream, whipped
6 tablespoons skinned hazelnuts, toasted and chopped
finely grated rind of 1 orange
6 teaspoons Grand Marnier

Bring the milk and cream to the boil, then add the chocolate and stir until melted. Set aside.

Heat the sugar with 1 tablespoon water to make a syrup. When the sugar has melted, bring to the boil and boil for 1 minute. Start to whisk the egg yolks, then gradually pour the syrup over the yolks while whisking continuously. Once the sugar has been incorporated, continue to whisk until the mixture is cold. The mixture will double in volume. Fold in the whipped cream.

Mix the egg mixture with the chocolate sauce. Distribute the mixture between the bowls. Sprinkle toasted chopped hazelnuts and grated orange zest over the top and drizzle sparingly with Grand Marnier. Chill well and serve with the ice-cream of your choice.

Cantaloupe Soup

This American soup is from a recipe by the late Robin Howe, published in the International Wine & Food Society's Guide to Soups. This famous cookery writer travelled widely, studying local cuisines whenever she went. This book, published in 1967, is 'before its time' in terms of the range of recipes it contains: there is a whole chapter on sweet soups! The gentleman from the International Food & Wine Society didn't think that Robin would have approved of our chocolate garnish – try it and see what you think.

PREPARATION AND COOKING TIME: 40 minutes
SERVES: 6

flesh of 1 large cantaloupe melon, about 1½ Kg (3lb 5oz)
50g (2oz) butter
1 tablespoon sugar
finely grated rind of 1 lemon
good pinch of salt
900ml (1½ pints) milk

SUGGESTED GARNISH:
3 tablespoons diced cantaloupe melon
shavings of bitter chocolate

Take enough of the melon flesh to cut 3 tablespoons of diced melon. Coarsely chop the remaining melon. Melt the butter and cook the coarsely chopped melon, sugar, lemon rind and salt gently for a few minutes. Add the milk, cover, bring to the boil and simmer gently for 15 minutes. Cool a little, then purée in a liquidiser or pass through a fine sieve. Chill well. Garnish each serving with diced melon shavings of bitter chocolate.

from The International Wine & Food Society's Guide to Soup, Robin Howe, 1967

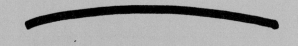

Peach Soup Flambé

Yes, now even soup can be flambéed! If you want to really excite your guests, this fascinating soup is the one for you. The vivid blue flames are impressive but the flavour of rosemary, honey and peaches combined brings to mind a decadent feast from Greek mythology.

PREPARATION AND COOKING TIME: 1 hour
SERVES: 6

> 1.35 kg (3lb) ripe peaches or nectarines
> 110g (4oz) sugar, plus 4 teaspoons
> 4 tablespoons lemon juice
> 1 tablespoon honey
> 1 teaspoon finely chopped fresh rosemary
> 2 tablespoon soured cream

TO GARNISH:
2 tablespoons soured cream
3 tablespoons Cognac or Armagnac

Pour 2 litres (3½ pints) water into a large pan and bring to the boil. Add the peaches and simmer for 5-15 minutes to loosen their skins, depending on their ripeness. Remove the peaches and set aside to cool. Reserve 150ml (¼ pint) of the cooking water. Peel the peaches, cut them in half and remove the stones.

Put 110g (4oz) sugar and 275ml (½ pint) water into a saucepan over a gentle heat. The aim is to dissolve the sugar before the liquid comes to the boil. Once dissolved, bring the liquid to the boil and boil for 1 minute. Add 6 peach halves and poach very gently for 15 minutes. Cool in the liquid.

Put the remaining peaches into a separate saucepan with the lemon juice, honey, rosemary and 3 teaspoons of the remaining sugar. Simmer gently, stirring frequently, for 10 minutes. Cool a little, then purée the mixture in a liquidiser. Reheat gently and stir in 2 tablespoons of soured cream.

Ladle the purée into soup bowls. Drain the peach halves and float cut side up in the centre of each bowl. Mix the soured cream for the garnish with the remaining sugar, then spoon the mixture over the peach halves. Warm the Cognac or Armagnac and spoon over the peaches. Dim the lights, ignite the brandy and serve the soup with the flames dancing.

From THE GOOD COOK: Soups © Time-Life Books B.V.

(V)

Strawberry Soup

This soup was originally produced for a successful PR exercise – to serve in front of the many TV cameras, to people queueing for the tennis at Wimbledon. However, a lot of trouble went into getting the recipe exactly right so we could launch it at a later date. Not as you would imagine from its colour, a sweet strawberry milkshake-like drink for children, but instead a not over-sweet soup with added wine for sophistication that should be eaten outside on a summer night when the underage contingent has gone to bed.

PREPARATION AND COOKING TIME: 3 hours 20 minutes
SERVES: 6

1 teaspoon grated orange rind
3 teaspoons caster sugar
275ml (½ pint) Australian Riesling
450g (1lb) strawberries, cut into fine slivers
              from top to tail
150ml (¼ pint) vanilla yoghurt

Infuse the orange rind, sugar and Australian Riesling for 1 hour. Strain through a fine sieve. Put into a bowl with the strawberries and marinate for 2 hours. Remove and reserve the strawberries and stir the wine into the yoghurt to the required dilution and potency! Return the strawberrie to the mixture and serve.

Barolo Blackberry Soup

Advertising Planner turned photographer Avril O'Reilly, got this recipe from her mum in Ireland. Mrs O'Reilly is a Pioneer, the Irish equivalent of a teetotaller, and supposedly hasn't touched a drop in all the 26 years that Avril has known her. However, ever since someone poured Baileys over her ice-cream in 1981, she has been looking for ways to work alcohol into food! If you are going to eat this blissful, deep purple combination of fruit and red wine hot with ice-cream, Avril recommends Häagen-Daz Vanilla because it's the hardest ice-cream and melts more slowly.

PREPARATION AND COOKING TIME : 15 minutes
SERVES : 6

> 700g (1½lb) blackberries
> 5 tablespoons sugar
> 450 ml (¾ pint) Barolo wine,
>   or any other full bodied red wine
> 1 cinnamon stick
> 2 strips of orange zest

TO GARNISH:
vanilla ice cream

Put all the ingredients into a saucepan and bring to the boil. Simmer very gently for 8 minutes. Serve warm or chilled with vanilla ice cream.

Sour Cherry Soup

Always the innovators, we launched this classic chilled sweet soup recipe on to the market in the summer of 1991. After lots of persuasion, several supermarkets agreed to stock what was considered to be rather an oddball product. 'Delicious with ice-cream, wonderfully refreshing,' we said 'Can't fail with all the hot weather we've been having...' As soon as it reached the shelves, the heavens opened and poured forth for what seemed like forty days and forty nights: sales plummeted. Proof that quality isn't always reflected in sales.

PREPARATION AND COOKING TIME: 15 minutes
SERVES: 6

550g (1¼ lb) fresh sour cherries, pitted, or 3 x 310g (11oz) jars of preserved Morello cherries, drained
75g (3oz) caster sugar, or to taste
1 tablespoon lemon juice
450ml (¾ pint) dry white wine
725ml (1¼ pints) water, including the juice from the jars if used
1 teaspoon ground cinnamon
150ml (¼ pint) single cream

TO GARNISH:
reserved cherry halves
150 ml (¼ pint) soured cream

Reserve 18 cherries and cut in half. Put the remaining cherries, sugar, lemon juice, white wine and water into a saucepan. Cover, bring to the boil and simmer gently for 5-10 minutes. Add the cinnamon, cool a little, then purée in a liquidiser. Stir in the single cream. Chill well.
Serve garnished with a few cherry halves and a swirl of soured cream.

Avril Jacobs' Hot Fruit Soup

When tasting this recipe for the book, Caroline Jeremy, had vivid recollections of her childhood in South Africa, the delicious fresh fruit and her mother's cooking. Mrs Jacobs got this recipe from a South African newspaper many years ago. She recalls that the recipe was from a small hotel on Du Toits Kloof near Cape Town which has since sadly burnt down. The hotel proprietor used to keep a pan of water with orange and lemon slices and cinnamon simmering on the hob to send delicious smells wafting through the rooms. Making this soup will have the same effect on your kitchen: perfect for winter entertaining.

PREPARATION AND COOKING TIME: 25 minutes
SERVES: 6

25g (1oz) butter
finely pared rind and juice of 2 lemons
finely pared rind and juice of 2 oranges
2 cinnamon sticks
10 cloves
10 apricots, halved and stoned
3 pears, peeled, cored and sliced
4 peaches, peeled, halved, stoned and sliced
4 tablespoons brandy
4 tablespoons port
1 apple, peeled, halved, cored and sliced
150g (5oz) white seedless grapes
1 small pineapple, skin removed and
    cut into small pieces
175g (6oz) cherries, stoned

Melt the butter and stir in the pared rind of the lemons and oranges, the cinnamon sticks and cloves. Cook gently for 2 minutes. Add the apricots, pears and peaches and cook for 2 minutes. Add the brandy and ignite with a match. When the flames have subsided, add the port, apple, grapes, pineapple, cherries, lemon and orange juice. Cover and simmer very gently for 10 minutes. Remove the rind, cinnamon sticks and cloves and serve with ice-cream.

Gooseberry Soup

Hungary is famous for its fruit soups and this one was bought to my attention by Victor Szwed, originally from Estonia, who works in our factory at Hythe Road. It originates from one of his Hungarian recipe books but he says he never sticks to the recipes and always adapts them for his dinner parties. Like many people who work in the soup factory, Victor does not often feel like making soup for his guests. However, this recipe is almost like a light mousse so it's acceptable.

PREPARATION AND COOKING TIME : 20 minutes
SERVES : 6

950g (2lb) under-ripe gooseberries, or if unavailable use
     gooseberries preserved in syrup or frozen gooseberries
pinch of salt
4 level dessertspoons sugar, or to taste
finely grated rind of 1 lemon
2 teaspoons plain flour
275ml (½ pint) milk
150ml (¼ pint) soured cream

Put the gooseberries into a large saucepan. Add a dash of water, the salt, sugar and lemon rind, cover and simmer gently until the gooseberries are tender. Cool a little, then purée in a liquidiser with the flour and pass through a sieve. Return to a clean saucepan, stir in the milk and soured cream, adding a little more milk if necessary to achieve the right consistency. Cover and simmer very gently for 5 minutes. Serve well chilled.

HOW TO MAKE THIS BOOK YOUR OWN

The design of this book was partly inspired by the scrapbooks kept by amateur cooks into which favourite recipes are stuck and written. These treasured scrapbooks are passed down from generation to generation and the recipes within are all guaranteed to work and taste delicious. The preceding recipes all come from somebody else's recipe scrapbook _ even those that are now produced by the soup company originated that way. We know they work and taste wonderful because we have spent weeks tasting them. But why take our word for it...

SOUP	Date cooked:	Cooking Notes:	Tasting notes:
Eg: Black-Eyed Bean with Oregano	24. 9. 96	Added a little more water, halfway through simmering	Delicious, substantial would do for a meal.
Arbroath Smokie and Scottish Cheddar			
Aubergine with Red Pepper Cream			
Aussie Roo			
Avocado and Cucumber			
Avocado Gazpacho			
Avril Jacobs' Hot Fruit			
Barolo Blackberry			
Black-Eyed Bean with Oregano			
Brussels Sprout and Chesnut			
Callaloo with Coconut			
Carrot & Coriander			
Celery and Cashew Nut			
Celery and Lemon Vichyssoise with Prawns			
Celery and Potato with Cheese			
Cheese with Crispy Bacon			
Chicory			
Chocolate			
Clam Chowder			
Clear Beef with Zupfnockerl			

SOUP	Date cooked:	Cooking Notes:	Tasting notes:
Crab Bisque			
Crab Creole			
Cream of Celeriac			
Cream of Chicken with Lemon and Tarragon			
Cream of Fennel			
Duck Noodle			
Florentine Bean			
Gazpacho			
Ginger and Carrot with Lime			
Gooseberry			
Goulash			
Grandad Elf's Spring Herb			
Green Pea, Lettuce and Mint			
Hamisha Chicken			
Iced Cucumber and Yoghurt			
Italian Peasant			
Jane Dodd's Borscht			
Jason Stead's Courgette and Brie			
Jerusalem Artichoke and Carrot			
Jerusalem Artichoke and Spinach			
Jewish Chicken			
Kohlrabi with Caraway			
Lamb and Irish Guinness			

SOUP	Date cooked:	Cooking Notes:	Tasting notes:
Lamb Tagine			
Lamb and Rowan with Ale			
Leek and Orange			
Lentil and Lemon			
Lentil and Tomato with Cumin and Coriander			
Lettuce and Lovage			
Fresh Lobster and Leek or Brot Giomach ùr Argus Leigis			
Mangetout			
Moroccan Chicken and Lemon			
Moroccan Chickpea and Spinach			
Moules Marinière			
Mrs Kendall's Lentil			
Mrs Mackay's Scotch Broth			
Mushroom with Parsley and Garlic			
Mussel, Red Pepper and Tomato			
Mustard and Cress			
National Trust Wild Mushroom			
Nettle			
New England Carrot, Apricot and Sesame			
New Zealand 'Kumara' or Sweet Potato Chowder			
Nick's Game and Chestnut			
Nora Carey's Ajiaco Bogotano			
Onion Panade			

SOUP	Date cooked:	Cooking Notes:	Tasting notes:
Pappa al Pomodoro			
Peach Flambé			
Persian Yoghurt			
Pumpkin			
Puy Lentil with Thyme			
Raspberry and Cranberry			
Ratatouille			
Real Dutch Pea			
Red Pepper and Goats' Cheese			
Rich Miso with Garlic			
Roasted Butternut Squash			
Roasted Garlic, Turnip and Chervil			
Roasted Parsnip and Parmesan			
Roasted Red Pepper, Corn and Chilli Chowder			
Roasted Tomato and Red Pepper			
Roasted Tomato with Basil Purée			
Robin Howe's Cantaloupe			
Russian Vegetable			
Fresh Salmon, Tomato and Basil			
Salsify with Mustard Seed			
Sherba			
Smoked Haddock Chowder			
Sorrel			

SOUP	Date cooked:	Cooking Notes:	Tasting notes:
Sorrel and Oyster			
Soupe au Pistou			
Soupe de Poissons			
Sour Cherry			
Sousboontjie			
Spicy Vegetable with Peanut			
Spinach with Nutmeg			
Split Pea and Leek			
Strawberry			
Summer Tomato			
Sweet Potato and Avocado			
Sweet Potato with Orange			
Tomato and Tarragon			
Ttoro Basque			
Turkey and Cranberry			
Tuscan Bean			
Twitcher's Tail			
Venison			
Vichyssoise			
White Bean, Tomato and Sage			
Additional Notes			

BIBLIOGRAPHY

Bareham, Lindsey: *A Celebration of Soup,* Michael Joseph, 1993

Bissell, Frances: *Sainsbury's Book of Food,* Websters International Publishers, 1989

Carey, Nora: *Perfect Preserves,* Stewart, Tabori & Chang, 1990

Castle, Coralie: *Soup,* Pitman Publishing, 1976

Forbes, Leslie: *A Table in Tuscany,* Webb and Bower, 1985

Gray, Rose and Rogers, Ruth: *The River Cafe Cook Book,* Ebury Press, 1995

Grigson, Sophie: *Sophie Grigson's Meat Course,* Network books, 1995

Harris, Valentina: *Italian Regional Cookery,* 1990

Howe, Robin: *The International Wine and Food Society's Guide to Soups,* The Wine and Food Society Publishing Company, 1967

Larousse Gastronomique: Mandarin, 1988

Torres, Marimar: *Catalan Country Kitchen,* Boxtree 1995

The Good Cook/Techniques and Recipes Series - Soups, Time Life, 1979

Wright, Hannah: *Soups,* Robert Hale, 1985

Index